HOUSING AND HEALTH

HOUSING AND HEALTH

STELLA LOWRY MB BSc

Assistant editor
British Medical Journal

with a historical background by

W F BYNUM MD PhD

Head of the Academic Unit
Wellcome Institute for the History of Medicine

Based on articles published in
the *British Medical Journal*

Published by the British Medical Journal
Tavistock Square, London WC1H 9JR

First published 1991

British Library Cataloguing in Publication Data
Lowry, Stella
  Housing and health.
  1. Health. Effects of housing
  I. Title
  363.5
ISBN 0–7279–0304–7

Filmset and printed in Great Britain by
Latimer Trend & Company Ltd, Plymouth

Contents

Acknowledgements

I am grateful to Dr Bill Bynum, head of the academic unit of the Wellcome Institute for the History of Medicine, for providing a fascinating historical background to the subject of housing and health, which constitutes the first chapter of this book.

I thank the following agencies for the use of their photographs: Barnabys, J Allan Cash, Mary Evans Picture Library, Format, Inside Housing/James A Gardiner, Frank Lane, Mansell Collection, Rick Matthews, Network, Photo Co-op, Popperfoto, Adrian Stevens, Thames Water, and Topham Picture Library.

The historical background

W F BYNUM

The great relevance to health of the immediate human environment has long been appreciated, and doctors have often had opinions on the ideal characteristics of that most important of environments, the house. The *locus classicus* of medical environmentalism, the Hippocratic treatise entitled *Airs, Waters and Places*, did not discuss individual dwellings, but its comments about the best kind of place to site a city recognised the unhealthiness of badly drained marshy areas or those exposed to extremes of wind and temperature.[1] In Roman times, Vitruvius offered considerable advice about the architectural features of comfortable and healthy houses, and the Romans developed a system of building codes, particularly in Rome where apartments were often several stories high and overcrowded tenements were common.[2]

Building codes were enacted for mediaeval London and covered such items as building materials and the prescribed thickness of party walls; the ever present dangers of fire or collapsed structures were the principal disasters that the regulations sought to prevent. Additional proclamations issued during Tudor and Stuart times touched such matters as the manufacture of brick, building heights, and the subdivision of existing houses into smaller units. Enforcement was at best variable, and any really grandiose schemes to rebuild London after the great fire of 1666 were hampered by a combination of economic restraints and property rights. Sunlight had hardly been at a premium in ancient Greece, and though it might have been expected to be in Britain, the window tax passed in the late seventeenth century and not repealed until the mid-nineteenth, encouraged neither light nor fresh air in domestic spaces.

Various Continental doctors from Johann Struppius (1530–1606) to Johann Peter Frank (1745–1821) included housing in their public health programmes[2] but, as Witold Rybczynski's evocative *Home: a Short History of an Idea* reminds us, privacy, comfort, and efficiency are not notions readily associated with the dwellings of earlier centuries.[3]

Housing as a sustained and specific medical issue is thus of relatively recent origin; even so it may be difficult to approach direct. The index to Sir George Newman's classic *The Building of a Nation's Health* (1929) contains, despite the reverberations of the book's title, only two brief references to housing. *The Oxford Companion to Medicine* (1986) has entries on Home, Sir Everard, home helps, home nursing, housemaid's knee, house mites, and house officer, but nothing specifically on where we live and why it matters.

Indirectly, of course, each of these books deals with the subject of housing and health under such topics as sanitation, water supply, sewage disposal, or simply public health. Poverty and overcrowding are two further variables that nineteenth century reformers also used in analysing disease and its prevention, and both were specifically related to housing. Housing is thus simultaneously ubiquitous and tantalisingly elusive as a historical public health issue, a subject more likely to be tackled by social, economic, or architectural historians than by medical ones.[4][5] As W M Frazer remarked, "It is indeed remarkable that during the first half of the nineteenth century parliament should have been willing to devote so much of its attention to factory legislation and to neglect to such an extent the equally or more important question of housing."[6]

Despite Frazer's reasoned judgment, it was during that very half century that the housing problem was perceived in its modern guise. Three factors led to this perception: the gigantic increase in the size of the problem, the widespread development of the tools and mentalities to describe social variables numerically, and the direct personal interest of several people who wished to implement aspects of a preventive ideal.

On the face of it, the problem was simple: the population of England and Wales doubled between the first census of 1801 and the Great Exhibition (and sixth census) of 1851, from just under nine million to just under 18 million. Such a massive increase in population would have inevitably, it seems, put an equally massive strain on the nation's housing stock, especially as the growth was almost entirely urban. London lived up to its reputation as the great wen, but many other places—such as, Manchester, Leeds, Birmingham, and Sheffield—were transformed from relatively small towns to substantial urban areas. Urban poverty could be infinitely more cruel than rural. In the countryside poaching, scavenging fuel and things to eat, growing vegetables, or keeping a pig could protect people from the worst ravages of subsistence living. In the new industrial cities, with a wage economy, uncertainties about employment, and often a surplus of labourers, life could be harsher. Surprisingly, the overall ratio of houses to people did not noticeably diminish, though the tendency of the middle and elite artisan classes to occupy more domestic space meant that many of what Edwin Chadwick (1800–90) called the "labouring population" were forced into densely packed and substandard accommodation.[7] It was this overcrowded and vulnerable residuum that came into sharper focus for sanitary reformers. Indicatively, the word "slum" entered the English language in the early nineteenth century.[4]

If these reformers ever doubted what their eyes would have told them, they had a set of tools that could lay out the issue in stark and revealing columns: social statistics. The early Victorian period coincided with the establishment of several local statistical societies that were filled with people keen to understand various medical and social phenomena in numerical terms. In 1837 William Farr (1807–83) introduced the civil registration of births and deaths, which provided a central office where vital statistics were collected, tabulated, and analysed. From the earliest days these figures told their grim tale of higher death rates in urban districts and, within those areas, among people living in conditions of overcrowded poverty. Common lodging houses were especially pernicious. In Bethnal Green, in the east end of London, Chadwick reported that professional men and their families lived to an average age of 45, whereas working class people and their families could expect an average of 16 years of life.[7] Bethnal Green was simply one of many localities where the same striking pattern could be, and was, discovered.

It was not simply an armchair revelation: Chadwick and his reformist minded colleagues saw much for themselves, made door to door surveys, and had their Victorian sensibilities shocked at the squalor and indecency that they found. Multiple families were

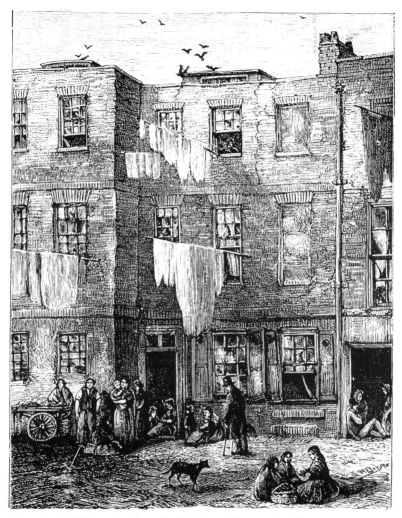

Overcrowded Victorian slums had obvious effects on health

living in single rooms; beds were continuously occupied by people of all ages and both sexes; birth, death, and copulation were visibly herded together. Reformers like Chadwick, Thomas Southwood Smith (1788–1861), and Hector Gavin (1815–55) came and saw and, more important in the long run, their campaign managed to

4

get through Parliament legislation that, almost as a byproduct, created its own cadre of professional sanitary, factory, and other kinds of inspectors. One historical model of social reform in the period argues that the mere investigation of comparatively unimportant matters regularly started cycles whereby new problems were uncovered, which required new legislation—and new inspectors to ensure its implementation. Historians have debated whether Professor MacDonagh's model fits the standard pattern of the growth of Victorian social legislation, but it has much to commend it.[8]

In many ways, however, housing remained legislatively sacrosanct compared with factories and other work places, and subjects of public interest, such as the lighting and paving of streets. Chadwick had his own grand scheme for public health: clean running water and the disposal of sewage under pressure through impervious glazed pipes. Much of the necessary work would have to be done outside the walls of houses, but at least the sinks and privies were inside. Landlords were therefore able to resist on the grounds that the added costs would raise rents and force impoverished tenants on to the streets or into workhouses. The finding by John Snow (1813–58) that cholera is waterborne provided a weapon for people who wanted private water companies to draw their water from sources free from contamination by sewage; and in 1855–75 in London the great engineering scheme of Joseph Bazalgette (1819–91) created the Thames embankment and the main London sewage system. Other cities followed suit with their own water and sewage systems. The municipalisation of the last private water companies early in this century was hailed widely as a triumph of public benefit over commercialism. *Autres temps, autres moeurs.*

Important as they were, water supply and sewage disposal represented only part of the housing issue. The continued rapid growth in population, particularly in urban areas, kept pressure on the housing stock, and increases in rents often outstripped any gains in wages. Subdividing already cramped flats or taking in lodgers could help the family exchequer at the expense of privacy, decency, and often health. For the evicted and homeless, the spectre of the workhouse loomed.

The Victorians mounted two primary responses, one legislative, the other philanthropic. Beginning with the Common Lodging

5

Houses Act 1851 and the Labouring Classes Lodging Houses Act 1851, both introduced by Lord Ashley (later the Earl of Shaftesbury), some regulation started to be enforced in the sector of the housing market that had been identified as being the least salubrious. The first of these acts allowed local authorities to inspect and supervise, and the second to operate at their own expense, lodgings for working class families. Many of the people affected by these acts were Irish and appropriately an Irish member of parliament, William Torrens (1813–94), shepherded through the act—still known by his name—that was the clear turning point in housing legislation. The Torrens Act 1868 made it the duty of householders to keep their properties in good repair. More important, if they did not do so the local authority could, on the recommendation of the medical officer of health or the application of four householders, close the properties or repair them at the expense of the owners. This act, and its subsequent modifications, has provided the basis of statutory powers relating to health and housing.[6]

Housing also attracted some philanthropic attention, most famously perhaps through the Peabody Trust of 1862, established by an American merchant, George Peabody (1795–1869), who ultimately made £500 000 available to build model homes.[9] At the same time, "five per cent philanthropy" described the movement whereby investors sought to do well by doing good in providing relatively low cost model housing for selected tenants.[10] The idea—often realised—was that sensible housing could be let, at a reasonable profit, on sensible terms. Model towns, such as Port Sunlight near Liverpool and New Earswick outside York, were more grand attempts to create healthy communities for sober workers.[5] These visible enterprises should not obscure the equally sober fact that, before the first world war, less than 1% of the nation's housing stock had been supplied by municipal and philanthropic activity.[9]

This was to change after the first world war with the promise of "homes fit for heroes". Almost one third of the dwellings erected between the wars were built by local authorities, a fact that people interested in public health, like W M Frazer, could survey with satisfaction. More than 40 years of the National Health Service, a consumer revolution, and the systematic privatisation of national investments, including council housing, would have provided much food for thought for the architects of the modern welfare

William McCullagh Torrens, MP (1813–94)

state. It can be argued that only some aspects of housing are actually medical; housing in the mass is an economic, social, or ultimately political issue. It can also be argued that the great German pathologist, Rudolf Virchow (1821–1902), was right to insist that "Medicine is a social science, and politics nothing else but medicine on a large scale."[11] If charity begins at home so too does health.

1 Hippocrates. *Airs, waters and places.* Cited in: Glacken C J. *Traces on the Rhodian shore.* Berkeley: University of California Press, 1967.
2 Caspari-Rosen B, ed. Cities and houses. *Ciba Symp* 1945;7:134–64.
3 Rybczynski W. *Home: a short history of an idea.* New York: Viking, 1986.
4 Wohl AS. *The eternal slum. Housing and social policy in Victorian London.* London: Edward Arnold, 1977.
5 Burnett J. *A social history of housing, 1815–1985,* 2nd ed. London: Methuen, 1986.
6 Frazer WM. *History of English public health, 1834–1939.* London: Baillière, Tindall and Cox, 1950.
7 Chadwick E. In: Flinn WM, ed. *Report on the sanitary condition of the labouring population of Great Britain.* Edinburgh: Edinburgh University Press, 1965. (First published in 1842.)
8 MacDonagh O. *Early Victorian government, 1830–1870.* London: Weidenfeld and Nicolson, 1977.
9 Daunton MJ. *House and home in the Victorian city. Working-class housing, 1850–1914.* London: Edward Arnold, 1983.
10 Tarn JN. *Five per cent philanthropy. An account of housing in urban areas between 1840 and 1914.* Cambridge: Cambridge University Press, 1973.
11 Ackerknecht E H. *Rudolf Virchow. Doctor, statesman, anthropologist.* Madison: University of Wisconsin Press, 1953:46.

Introduction

The connection between health and the dwellings of the population is one of the most important that exists

FLORENCE NIGHTINGALE

A recent World Health Organisation publication on housing and health mentioned the need to reduce the "cruel toll of death and disease directly attributable to the appalling living conditions of one quarter of the world's population."[1] We can all accept that living in shanty towns in the Third World can damage people's health, but many of us have forgotten how much housing can influence health in Britain.

Housing and public health

The Victorians explained the association between poor housing and ill health in terms of the miasmic theory—bad smells transmitted disease—but their solutions (slum clearance and improved sanitation) did improve health. Improvements in the death rates from infectious diseases like cholera and typhoid and, to some extent, tuberculosis owed more to improved standards of housing than to knowledge of microbiology and the development of antibiotics.[2]

The Victorians took a broad view of health. Their attempts to reduce overcrowding in slums were prompted largely by outrage at the potential harm to mental and moral "health" of inadequate separation of the sexes, but the results reduced the spread of infectious illness. Housing had a central role in the development of the public health movement.[3][4]

In 1918 there was an outcry when it was discovered that 41% of conscripts were of medical grade C3—unfit for military service. There were calls for improved public health, including better

9

housing. After the war houses were in short supply—600 000 too few by the armistice, and over 800 000 by 1921—and a huge building programme began. The solid, well constructed semi-detached houses with private gardens and indoor bathrooms built in the 1920s and 1930s really were the promised "homes fit for heroes." Indeed, they still compare favourably with many of the houses built since.

Never mind the quality

As the slums were cleared, partly for rebuilding and partly through bombing during the second world war, the emphasis shifted from quality to quantity. The trend reached its peak in the 1960s, when vast rapid build projects sprang up. Builders were given financial incentives to use new, and largely untested, building techniques; and thousands of people were housed in the preformed concrete blocks that resulted.

A period of relative complacency followed. The housing crisis seemed to be over. The baby boom had finished, and housing no longer topped the political agenda. Then the complaints began. The new houses were not structurally sound. They were hard to heat, prone to damp, and filled with asbestos. There was nowhere

A huge building programme after the first world war produced thousands of "homes fit for heroes"

Emphasis on quantity rather than quality

for children to play, rubbish accumulated in walkways, and graffiti flourished on walls. Despite such visible deterioration people were slow to look for effects of modern housing on health.

Doctors and housing

Housing still influences our health. Houses should provide basic health requirements like shelter, warmth, sanitation, and privacy, and badly designed or dangerously constructed houses can directly damage residents' health. Doctors need to know to what extent their patients' illnesses are the result of their living conditions, and whether anything can be done to improve them.

Hospital doctors are increasingly expected to use day case techniques and early discharge. General practitioners are being asked to manage more and more conditions largely or solely in the community. These trends can be followed safely only if the home

11

conditions of each patient are well known and the probable effects of these are understood.

People with health problems (such as the elderly, the handicapped, and the chronically sick) may have specific housing needs. Doctors are often asked to help patients obtain rehousing on medical grounds, and they need to understand how this system works if they are to make the best use of it.

Perhaps the most important reason that doctors should know about housing is that they are in a position to influence change. A BMA book on deprivation and ill health summed up that responsibility: "Doctors are responsible for promoting health as well as treating illness, and doctors share with other disciplines a responsibility to suggest social policies which might prevent avoidable illness."[5]

Blame the victim

There has been a change of emphasis in public health in the 1970s and 1980s. Health issues have become individualised—people should stop smoking, eat less fat, use condoms, not share needles, have regular cervical smears. Even the campaigns to prevent hypothermia have degenerated into an obsession with individual behaviour: stay in one warm room, wear several layers of clothes, and knit yourself a woolly hat.

Of course people should know how their behaviour affects their health, but we have become so obsessed with individual responsibility that we have stopped looking at how more widespread intervention might help. Perhaps with a prime minister who claimed that "there is no such thing as society" this is not too surprising. As Cathy McCormack of the Easthall Residents Association in Glasgow puts it, "Blame the victim syndrome is the worst disease we know."

But things are changing. Architects and planners now accept that many of the problems of concrete slab blocks are caused by genuine faults in the design. A vast number of people live in homes that are well nigh impossible to keep warm and dry, and the effects on their health are slowly being recognised. Many old properties are in desperate need of maintenance work. Increasing numbers of people are visibly homeless. The complacency of the '70s and early

'80s is fading, and housing is emerging as a major public health issue again.

Science and common sense

The effects of housing on health are difficult to study. Common sense tells us that the relation exists, but it is usually impossible to prove it scientifically. Doctors who have come to expect p values and confidence intervals will be dismayed at the lack of hard science. The mass of confounding variables in each situation makes assessment of any one risk factor almost impossible. This lack of a firm association provides a useful loophole for governments that cannot or will not fund the remedial programmes needed.

In this book I look at some of the more important influences on housing and health in Britain today. I try to identify how much has been established by scientific investigation and how much by sensible observation, and discuss to what extent we should insist on hard evidence before demanding change. I hope that this will provide an introduction to the subject for young doctors who, like me, trained in the years of relative complacency and that it will also provide a useful update for those who have always appreciated the association between housing and health.

1 World Health Organisation. *Housing and health. An agenda for action.* Geneva: WHO, 1987.
2 Cartwright FF. *A social history of medicine.* London: Longman, 1977.
3 Jacobs M, Stevenson G. Health and housing: a historical examination of alternative perspectives. *Int J Health Services* 1981;1:105–22.
4 Ormandy D. Historical development of housing hygiene policy. *J R Soc Health* 1987;**107**:39–42.
5 British Medical Association, Board of Science and Education. *Deprivation and ill health.* London: BMA, 1987.

Temperature and humidity

Most people believe that living in a cold damp house is bad for their health. The dangers of hypothermia in elderly people are well known, but how much are other people affected by temperature? How serious are the risks and how can we reduce them? (For practical purposes we do not need to consider excessive heat in reviewing housing and health in Britain, although very low humidity can cause irritation of mucous membranes and may predispose to respiratory tract infections.)

The idea that cold conditions are bad for health gets some support from the finding of an excess mortality in winter in Britain. Excess winter mortality is the difference between the number of deaths in the four winter months and the average of the numbers in the preceding autumn and following spring. A recent analysis shows that for each degree Celsius by which the winter is colder than average there are about 8000 excess deaths.[1] The figure shows the seasonal variations in mortality.

About 40 000 more people die in Britain in the winter than in the summer, and most of them are elderly. Very few of these excess deaths, however, are due to hypothermia—most are from respiratory and cardiovascular diseases. A recent report to the Building Research Establishment concluded that defining a safe limit for house temperatures was impossible, but the risks as temperature falls can be summarised (box).[2]

Affordable warmth

The Parker Morris standard has been used to set minimum temperatures for dwellings,[3] but since 1980 there has been no

14

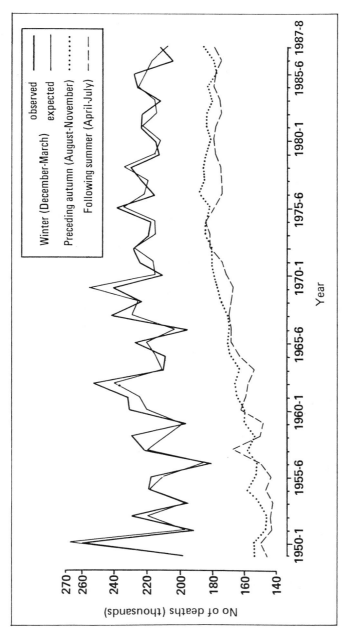

Seasonal mortality 1949–88. (Reproduced from Population Trends 1988; 5:18 (crown copyright))

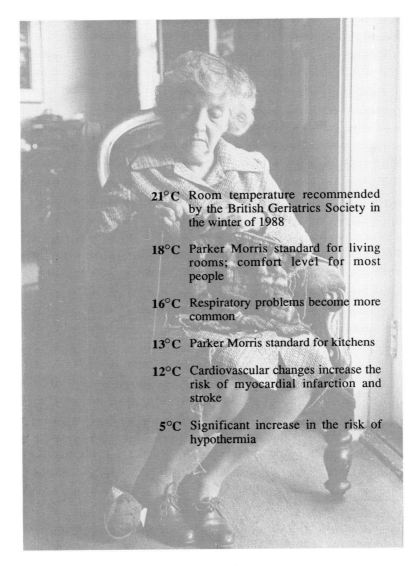

21°C Room temperature recommended by the British Geriatrics Society in the winter of 1988

18°C Parker Morris standard for living rooms; comfort level for most people

16°C Respiratory problems become more common

13°C Parker Morris standard for kitchens

12°C Cardiovascular changes increase the risk of myocardial infarction and stroke

5°C Significant increase in the risk of hypothermia

definition of what constitutes an acceptable indoor temperature. Even less attention has been given to how much people should be expected to spend on heating. Many families in Britain live in "fuel poverty," which occurs when people cannot afford to heat their homes adequately. It does not necessarily equate with absolute poverty, but the two often occur together.

Unemployed, chronically sick, and elderly people are among the poorest in Britain. These groups spend most of each day at home, and have to heat their houses for longer than other people. The most effective and efficient way of heating a house is by central heating, but the people who can least afford to waste money on inefficient systems are also those least likely to have centrally heated homes. Attempts to economise by heating only part of the house cause temperature differentials that encourage condensation and mould growth. This may be compounded by water production from the heating source—paraffin heaters are notorious for this. About 7% of homes in Britain are damp,[4] and damp houses are usually cold.

Fuel poverty exists because the people with least to spend on heating are often housed in the homes that are hardest to heat. Many low cost houses are prone to cold and damp. Through beams in slab block constructions act as cold bridges and reduce the insulation of external walls; ill fitting doors and windows cause excessive ventilation; precast concrete slabs have a high thermal mass and are difficult to heat—a room will only feel warm when the air in it and its fabric have warmed.[5]

The poor spend twice as much (as a percentage of their total income) as the rest of the population on heating (table). Boardman has suggested that fuel costs should not exceed 10% of the total household income.[6] Residents are often blamed for their damp living conditions. Washing and drying clothes increases the moisture content of a house by about 5·5 kg a day and moisture emission rises with the number of people in a dwelling,[7] but occupants can usually do little to reduce these factors. Sometimes the solutions offered are offensive as well as unhelpful, such as the following advice given to a Glasgow resident who complained that her flat was damp:

"Keep your windows open
when you make love. Heavy
breathing causes condensation,
you know."

TABLE—*Weekly expenditure on fuel per household in Britain in 1985*

	30% Of poorest households	Remaining 70% of households	Average
Actual amount spent (£)	8·06	10·76	9·95
Percentage of total income	11·0	5·4	6·1

Based on Boardman[6]

Cold damp homes and health

The dangers of very low indoor temperatures are well established, but it is harder to prove that at less extreme temperatures cold damp houses affect health. Several studies have found an association between damp housing and respiratory disease, particularly wheeze, in children,[8 9] and there is an association between asthma and sensitivity to allergens from moulds.[10] But not all studies have found simple relations between damp housing and poor health.

In 1986 Strachan and Elton found an association between parents' reports of damp and mould in the home and respiratory problems in their children,[11] but there was a poor correlation between reported wheezing and recorded consultations with the general practitioner for respiratory problems. The researchers concluded that reporting bias might be operating. Parents of children with wheeze may be more likely to notice poor conditions at home, or people in poor houses may be more likely to report illness in their children.

In later studies Strachan found a significant association between reports of visible mould in the home and reported wheeze but no association between reports of mould and objective measurements of bronchial reactivity.[12 13] He interpreted this as further support for the suggestion of reporting bias.

Self reported illness

A recent attempt to overcome the problem of reporting bias has been made by Martin and others in two studies in which environmental health officers surveyed houses for damp and mould independently of the assessment of the occupants' health.[14 15] Damp conditions were significantly associated with reports of respiratory illness in children, and were also associated with vomiting and aches and pains. The housing conditions did not correlate with reports of adult ill health. These studies contained objective assessments of the housing conditions and were controlled for social class, smoking, overcrowding, family income, and numbers of children in the home; but they still relied on self reporting of illness.

Strachan believes that self reporting is acceptable if the subject is unlikely to spot the hypothesis under test, but he believes that "It is difficult to mask an interest in the link between damp housing and respiratory illness." Martin believes that self reported illness is important. "People do not necessarily consult their doctor when they are ill. Health is much more than freedom from the need to consult a doctor." Certainly the WHO would agree with that.[16]

Conclusions

Living in cold damp houses affects people's health. This is true within a strictly medical model, but the problems are even more serious if we look at a wider definition of health, akin to the WHO concept of emotional and physical well being. At extremely low temperatures cardiovascular problems occur and the risk of hypothermia rises. Less severe cold conditions encourage condensation, and parents report more respiratory problems in their children if they live in damp houses. This probably reflects some increased morbidity in the children, and certainly an increased amount of stress in the parents. The psychological consequences of having to scrape mould off the walls of your home every day are obvious.

Comment

Ray Ranson, the WHO's housing hygiene consultant, believes that it is often easier to get funding for housing projects on grounds other than health. This should certainly be possible for cold damp homes, which deteriorate rapidly through corrosion, timber decay, and electrical problems and are expensive to maintain.

The problem of cold damp houses should be tackled because of its effect on health and its economic effects on the housing stock. Standards should be set so that an acceptable safe indoor tempera-

*Having to scrape mould off the walls of your home
every day is deleterious to psychological well being*

ture, say 20°C, can be achieved at no more than 10% of the
household income. Any excess needed should be provided in social
payments.

Although most houses can be made warm and dry if enough is
spent on heating, this is not the most economical solution. Where
possible, structural defects that promote cold and condensation
should be repaired so that properties can be brought up to the
standard. Measures such as fungicidal washes and paints should be
used only for temporary relief.[17] Public sector houses should be

improved with specially allocated funds, and grants should be available to encourage private owners to upgrade their properties. No family should be condemned to live in fuel poverty.

1   Curwen M, Devis T. Winter mortality, temperature and influenza: has the relationship changed in recent years? *Population Trends* 1988;**54**:17–20.
2   Mant DC, Gray JAM. *Building regulation and health.* Garston: Department of the Environment Building Research Establishment, 1986.
3   Parker M. *Homes for today and tomorrow.* London: HMSO, 1961. (Ministry of Housing and Local Government.)
4   Department of the Environment. *English house conditions survey 1986.* London: HMSO, 1988.
5   Markus TA. *Cold, condensation, climate and poverty in Glasgow.* Warwick: Legal Research Institute, University of Warwick, 1987. (Unhealthy housing: prevention and remedies.)
6   Boardman B. *Defining affordable warmth.* Warwick: Legal Research Institute, University of Warwick, 1987. (Unhealthy housing: prevention and remedies.)
7   Institution of Environmental Health Officers. *Background notes on condensation.* London: IEHO, 1983.
8   Burr ML, St Leger AS, Yarnell JWG. Wheezing, dampness, and coal fires. *Community Med* 1981;**3**:205–9.
9   Burr ML, Miskelly FG, Butland BK, Merrett TG, Vaughan-Williams E. Environmental factors and symptoms in infants at high risk of allergy. *J Epidemiol Community Health* 1989;**43**:125–32.
10 Burr ML, Mullins J, Merrett TG, Stott NCH. Indoor moulds and asthma. *J R Soc Health* 1988;**108**:99–101.
11 Strachan DP, Elton RA. Relationship between respiratory morbidity in children and the home environment. *Family Practice* 1986;**3**:137–42.
12 Strachan DP. Damp housing and childhood asthma; validation of reporting of symptoms. *Br Med J* 1988;**297**:1223–6.
13 Strachan DP, Sanders CH. Damp housing and childhood asthma; respiratory effects of indoor air temperature and relative humidity. *J Epidemiol Community Health* 1989;**43**:7–14.
14 Martin CJ, Platt SD, Hunt SM. Housing conditions and ill health. *Br Med J* 1987;**294**:1125–7.
15 Platt SD, Martin CJ, Hunt SM, Lewis CW. Damp housing, mould growth, and symptomatic health state. *Br Med J* 1989;**298**:1673–8.
16 World Health Organisation. Alma-Ata 1978; primary health care. Geneva: WHO, 1978. (Health for all series. No 1.)
17 Bravery AF, Grant C, Sanders CH. *Controlling mould growth in housing.* Warwick; Legal Research Institute, University of Warwick, 1987. (Unhealthy housing: prevention and remedies.)

Indoor air quality

Most people know that outdoor air pollution can damage their health, but few pay any attention to the quality of indoor air. Yet we spend about 80% of our time indoors, as much as three quarters of this in our own homes. Elderly people, mothers and young children, and the sick spend most time at home and may also be particularly sensitive to any effects of pollutants on health.

As fuel costs have risen people have tried to conserve energy by making their homes more airtight—using double glazing, cavity wall insulation, draught proofing, and loft insulation. But this also means that any contaminants are less diluted by incoming air. (Cavity wall insulation can even be a source of pollution as some types release formaldehyde.) In the 1960s asbestos was often used for lagging and insulating. Intact asbestos in houses is not a great problem, but a potential risk to health exists if the building becomes damaged or decayed, and the removal of asbestos from houses poses a serious risk.[1]

Assessing the risk

The health effects of indoor air pollutants are hard to study because people move from room to room and it is difficult to isolate the effects of individual agents. In adults occupational and smoking histories can confuse the picture. Moreover, what do you measure? Exposure to a pollutant depends on its concentration and how that varies with time and position. For some pollutants, such as radon, the average concentration and duration of exposure are important; for others the peak exposure is the key—for example, carbon monoxide production by a faulty heater.

Much of our knowledge about indoor air pollutants comes from studies of occupational exposure, but the concentrations are usually much greater in industry than in the home. Standards for industrial air may, however, be too lax for houses, where people may be particularly vulnerable.

The WHO has issued guidelines on how to monitor indoor air quality, including details of sampling techniques for different types of pollutant, and how to extrapolate from experiments in animals and studies of occupational exposure when assessing risks to health.[23] Ideally, studies of possible health effects of pollutants should include people selected because of their expected vulnerability—for example, those with cardiorespiratory problems.

Most people have heard of the sick building syndrome: vague symptoms such as irritation of the mucous membranes, headaches, fatigue, and nausea occurring without explanation in clusters associated with a particular, usually modern, building. This is an occupational health problem, and I will not discuss it in detail, but reviews of the subject do illustrate just how difficult it is to assess indoor air quality.[45]

Pollutants of indoor air

Microbial contamination of indoor air can damage health. The best known example is the association between exposure to house dust mite antigen and asthma.[6–9] Less common examples include legionnaires' disease and humidifier fever, which occur when there is microbial contamination of air heating or conditioning systems.[10 11] Occupants can themselves be a source of pollutants ranging from the hydrocarbons found in body odour to the chemicals released by cigarette smoking. Mant and Gray have listed some of the pollutants of indoor air, and their results are summarised in table I.[12]

The concentration of a pollutant depends on its rates of production and removal, where it comes from, and its dilution by ventilation. The quality of indoor air can be improved by increasing the ventilation, removing or modifying the source of pollution, cleaning the air, or changing the occupants' behaviour.

Assessing effects on health

Most of us are unaware of any ill effects from our indoor air. The most common problem in Britain is probably allergy to house dust

TABLE I—*Sources and effects of indoor air pollution*

Pollutant	Possible sources	Health effects
Carbon dioxide	Metabolic production by occupants; flueless combustion equipment	None known at concentrations found in homes
Carbon monoxide	Combustion of fossil fuels, including cigarettes	Anoxia; can be fatal
Nitrogen dioxide	Combustion of fossil fuels, including cigarettes	Animals show decreased resistance to bacterial infection; possible increase in respiratory tract infections in humans
Tobacco smoke		Irritation of mucous membranes; respiratory tract infections; lung cancer
Formaldehyde	Urea formaldehyde foam insulation; synthetic carpets; pressed wood products	Irritation of mucous membranes; possible carcinogen
Asbestos	Lagging material, cement	Lung cancer; mesothelioma
Microbes	Dust; mould; air conditioning systems	Allergies; infections
Radon	Soil gas	Lung cancer

mite antigen, and the greatest inconvenience is the need to vacuum clean regularly. A few people are so sensitive to air pollutants in their homes that they have to go to extreme lengths to reduce their exposure. These so called "chemically sensitive" people develop dermatological, respiratory, and central nervous system illnesses on exposure to pollutants, and the building industry, especially in North America, has developed techniques to prevent this. Installing airtight vapour barriers to prevent pollutants in the building shell entering the home, ensuring that all oil has been washed off any steel studs used, and avoiding all wood products, carpets, polyvinyl chloride tiles, and certain cements are among the measures used.[13]

It is one thing to show that a pollutant is present but quite another to prove that it is harmful. This is well illustrated in the studies by Melia and others of nitrogen dioxide in homes. They proved that gas cookers were important sources of nitrogen dioxide in indoor air[14] and found a trend for increasing reports of respiratory illness in children exposed to increasing indoor concentrations of nitrogen dioxide.[15 16] But the effects of social class, smoking, possible reporting bias, age of the child, and urban or rural setting all interacted with the effects of nitrogen dioxide concentration.

A recurring problem in studies of housing and health is that the effects of individual variables rarely reach significance. Even so, Ogston et al argue that when the trend is always in the direction of an association the findings are probably real: "There has been no significant negative association reported, although it would be expected on statistical grounds from at least one of the studies. This pattern of findings would fit better with a hypothesis that concerned a small but real effect."[17]

Radon

The recent scare stories that possibly hundreds of people are dying of lung cancer caused by radon gas in their homes show just how difficult it is to interpret information about indoor air pollution. Radon is a colourless odourless gas that is present in almost all rocks and soils, but particularly in granite. Radon emits high energy α particles during its decay to a stable isotope of lead, and these can damage the bronchial epithelium. Radon is the single largest source of exposure to radiation for most people in Britain

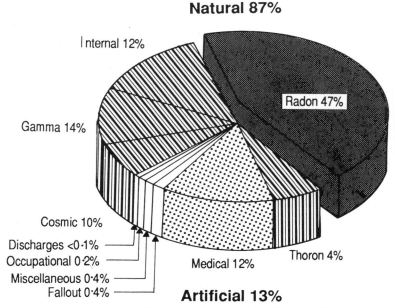

Average annual dose of radiation in Britain (2·5 mSv overall). (Based on information from the National Radiological Protection Board)

(figure).[18] Exposure to radon causes lung cancer in uranium miners,[19 20] and it acts synergistically with cigarette smoking. Some cases of myeloid leukaemia are thought to be caused possibly by domestic exposure to radon.[21] Using data from 15 countries, Henshaw *et al* found significant correlations between the incidence of myeloid leukaemia and the mean radon concentration and suggested that in Britain up to 12% of cases of myeloid leukaemia might be caused by radon. They failed, surprisingly, to find a correlation with the incidence of lung cancer. Their data about the incidence of cancer and the concentrations of radon were not always sampled from the same areas, which makes interpretation difficult. Previous studies have not shown an association between the incidence of leukaemia in uranium miners and exposure to radon.

Radon gets into homes from building materials and ground water, but the main source is soil gas. Higher indoor temperatures and the effects of wind on a building together lower the atmos-

Could these Cornish cottages damage your health?

pheric pressure inside compared with outside, and so soil gas flows into the building. Double glazing or draught proofing can raise the indoor concentration of radon by a third.

Because the indoor concentration of radon depends on the structure of a building as well as its site, it is impossible to estimate the radon concentration—it must be measured. Surveys of the radon concentration in homes across Britain have found great variation.[22][23] The mean annual effective dose equivalent in dwellings is 1000 µSv, but in parts of south west England the mean indoor concentration of radon is 15 times the national average.

In miners radon has undoubted effects,[20] but here the exposure is high. In some homes the concentration of radon exceeds that permitted in mines, but this does not prove that domestic exposure

27

is harmful. A greater minute volume in miners may produce an enhanced deposition rate of radon daughters in their lungs compared with an equivalent domestic exposure, as may the relative excess of radon daughters found in mine air or the presence of other contaminants in dust, which may act synergistically with radon. (A known hazard to healthy workers may, however, be even more dangerous to the sort of people exposed for prolonged periods at home.)

Models of the health risks from radon have been designed using information from industrial exposure, extrapolations from the effects of radiation in animal studies, data about survivors of atomic bombs, and information about patients treated with x radiation for ankylosing spondylitis between 1935 and 1954.[24][25] The National Radiological Protection Board has recently revised its estimates of the risk of developing lung cancer from domestic exposure to radon (table II).[26] It suggests that the national average domestic exposure of a concentration of 20 Bq/m^3 carries an estimated lifetime risk of 0·3%, which implies that one in 20 cases of lung cancer in Britain may be caused by domestic exposure to radon. Despite recent suggestions that radon is a major risk factor for lung cancer in the general population, however, no correlation exists between the distribution of mortality from lung cancer and domestic exposure to radon. The south west of England, which has the highest concentrations of radon, is a low risk area for lung cancer.

Homes in areas with high concentrations of radon in the soil can be built so as to minimise its entry into the building.[27] People living in houses with high indoor concentrations can get mortgages or discretionary home improvement grants to pay for sealing the

TABLE II—*National Radiological Protection Board's estimates of lifetime risk of developing lung cancer from lifelong exposure to radon at home*

Average concentration of radon (Bq/m³)	Lifetime risk (%)		
	Whole population	Smokers	Non-smokers
20	0·3	1	0·1
100	1·5	5	0·5
200	3·0	10	1·0
400	6·0	20	2·0

building from soil air.[28] The National Radiological Protection Board has revised its recommendations about which homes need remedial action in the light of the latest estimates of risk. Its recommended action concentration has been reduced from 400 to 200 Bq/m³, which it estimates will more than treble (to about 75 000, mainly in Devon and Cornwall) the number of homes needing treatment.[26] The board also recommends that parts of the country where 1% of homes are expected to exceed the action concentration should be designated as "affected areas". People living in affected areas would be advised to have the radon concentrations in their homes measured, and precautions against radon entry should be included in the design of new dwellings.

The Institution of Environmental Health Officers has called recently for changes in the law to introduce a system of radon certification of houses at the time of sale. It also wants environmental health officers to be able to serve statutory notice on landlords to remedy tenanted buildings found to be above the action level.[29] Yet despite so much concern from the government and professional organisations there are still no hard data proving that domestic exposure to radon is a major hazard to health.[30] It is easy for people to find out what their annual exposure to radon is (box), but difficult for them to know what to make of the results.

People living in areas associated with high concentrations of radon can have a free survey by writing to the National Radiological Protection Board Radon Survey, Chilton, Didcot, Oxfordshire OX11 0RQ. People living in other areas can also have a survey done by the National Radiological Protection Board but have to pay a fee of about £30. Various private companies offer radon surveys, but the sampling duration is usually much shorter than that offered by the National Radiological Protection Board and the results may not be so reliable.

Conclusion

Indoor air pollutants can affect health, but the pollutants present vary from house to house, and the concentrations required to cause harm depend on individual susceptibility. Radon is a known carcinogen in miners. Its concentration in homes varies widely and in some places exceeds the limits set for industrial exposure, but there is no direct evidence linking domestic exposure with an increased risk of lung cancer.

Comment

It is impossible to make recommendations about the quality of indoor air that will protect everyone, but some simple precautions do seem worth while. All domestic heating and cooking appliances should be correctly vented. Damp houses should be treated, as this discourages mites and mould growth and improves air quality. Modifications to make houses airtight should still allow occupants to vary the amount of ventilation.

Until studies are conducted to assess the link between individual lifetime exposure to radon and cause of death we should not overestimate the risks. For most of us, however, radon is the single largest source of exposure to radiation, and it seems sensible that the design of new houses should keep to the National Radiological Protection Board's recommendations. The expense of altering existing dwellings may not be justified, and public money might be better spent on tackling homelessness or fuel poverty.

1 People's Asbestos Action Campaign. *Asbestos fact pack*. 3rd ed. London: PAAC, 1987.
2 World Health Organisation Regional Office for Europe. *Indoor air pollutants: exposure and health effects*. Copenhagen: WHO, 1982.
3 World Health Organisation Regional Office for Europe. *Indoor air quality research*. Copenhagen: WHO, 1984.
4 Sykes JM. *Sick building syndrome: a review*. Bootle: Health and Safety Executive Technical Division, 1988.
5 Ashley S. Sick buildings. *Building Services* 1986; February: 25–30.
6 Blythe ME. Some aspects of the ecological study of the house dust mite. *Br J Dis Chest* 1976;70:3–31.
7 Burr ML, Dean BV, Merrett TG, Neale E, St Leger AS, Verrier-Jones ER. Effects of anti-mite measures on children with mite sensitive asthma: a controlled trial. *Thorax* 1980;35:506–12.
8 Burr ML, Neale E, Dean BV, Verrier-Jones ER. Effect of a change to mite-free bedding on children with mite-sensitive asthma: a controlled trial. *Thorax* 1980;35:513–14.
9 Kodama AM, McGee RI. Airborne microbial contaminants in indoor environments. Naturally ventilated and air-conditioned homes. *Archives of Environmental Health* 1986;41:306–11.
10 Sweet LC, Anderson JA, Callies QC, Coates EO. Hypersensitivity pneumonitis related to a home furnace humidifier. *J Allergy Clin Immunol* 1971;48:171–8.

11 Tourville DR, Weiss WI, Wertlake PT, Leudermann GM. Hypersensitivity pneumonitis due to contamination of a home humidifier. *J Allergy Clin Immunol* 1972;**49**:245–51.

12 Mant DC, Gray JAM. *Building regulation and health*. Garston: Building Research Establishment, Department of the Environment, 1986.

13 Olivier D. Housing the chemically sensitive. *Building Services* 1988; May: 47–8.

14 Goldstein BD, Melia RJW, Chinn S, Florey CV, Clark D, John HH. The relationship between respiratory illness in primary school children and the use of gas for cooking. II. Factors affecting nitrogen dioxide levels in the home. *Int J Epidemiol* 1979;**8**:339–45.

15 Melia RJW, Florey CV, Chinn S. The relationship between respiratory illness in primary school children and the use of gas for cooking. I. Results from a national survey. *Int J Epidemiol* 1979;**8**:333–8.

16 Florey CV, Melia RJ, Chinn S, *et al*. The relationship between respiratory illness in primary school children and the use of gas for cooking. III. Nitrogen dioxide, respiratory illness, and lung function. *Int J Epidemiol*. 1979;**8**:347–53.

17 Ogston SA, Florey CV, Walker CHM. The Tayside infant morbidity and mortality study: effect on health of using gas for cooking. *Br Med J* 1985;**290**:957–60.

18 Hughes JS, Shaw KB, O'Riordan MC. *Radiation exposure of the UK population—1988 review*. Chilton: National Radiological Protection Board, 1988.

19 Committee on the Biological Effects of Ionising Radiations, Board on Radiation Effects Research, Commission on Life Sciences, National Research Council. *Health risks of radon and other internally deposited alpha-emitters. BEIR IV*. Washington: National Academy Press, 1988.

20 Roscoe RJ, Steenland K, Halperin WE, Beaumont JJ, Waxweiler RJ. Lung cancer mortality among nonsmoking uranium miners exposed to radon daughters. *JAMA* 1989;**262**:629–33.

21 Henshaw DL, Eatough JP, Richardson RB. Radon as a causative factor in induction of myeloid leukaemia and other cancers. *Lancet* 1990;**335**:1008–12.

22 O'Riordan MC, James AC, Green BMR, Wrixon AD. *Exposure to radon daughters in dwellings*. Chilton: National Radiological Protection Board, 1987.

23 Wrixon AD, Green BMR, Lomas PR, *et al*. *Natural radiation exposure in UK dwellings*. Chilton: National Radiological Protection Board, 1988.

24 Thomas DC, McNeill KG, Dougherty C. Estimates of lifetime lung cancer risks resulting from Rn progeny exposure. *Health Physics* 1985;**49**:825–46.

25 Hendee WR, Doege TC. Origin and health risks of indoor radon. *Seminars in Nuclear Medicine* 1987;**18**:3–9.

26 O'Riordan MC. *Human exposure to radon in homes. Recommendations for the practical application of the Board's statement*. Chilton: National Radiological Protection Board, 1990.

27 Cliff KD. Radon remedies in dwellings. *Radiological Protection Bulletin* 1987;**79**:11–4.

28 Department of the Environment. *The householders' guide to radon*. London: HMSO, 1988.

29 Institution of Environmental Health Officers. *Radon. Report of the IEHO survey on radon in homes 1987/8*. London; IEHO, 1989.

30 Samet JM, Nero AV. Indoor radon and lung cancer. *N Engl J Med* 1989;**320**:591–4.

Sanitation

Sanitation has had, and continues to have, more impact on health than any advance in medical science. In developing countries over eight million children die from diarrhoeal illnesses each year because of poor sanitation,[1] and in nineteenth century Britain epidemics of cholera and typhoid were common until the introduction of clean drinking water and safe sewage disposal. Now we take good sanitation for granted. Yet recent incidents, such as the contamination of water with aluminium in Camelford in 1988 and revelations that British water does not meet European Community standards, have posed questions about the safety of our domestic water supply and our handling of waste. People in Britain use, on average, 130 litres of water a day each. How are standards maintained, and where can the systems break down?

Water quality

Until last year the only requirement of drinking water in Britain was that it should be "wholesome." Various guidelines had been issued by government departments and the WHO, but the Secretary of State for the Environment was the final arbiter of what constituted wholesome water. In 1980 the European Community issued a directive (80/778/EEC) about drinking water quality; it came into force fully in 1985. The British government decided that water quality would meet the standards of the directive if the average results of tests did so. (In the year ending June 1989 the failure rate in quality tests was less than two per thousand.) The community decided, however, that each and every sample must comply; hence the recent publicity about Britain's failure to reach European standards.[2]

The European Community directive lays down safe limits for a range of chemical and microbiological substances in water. There are 66 variables in all, and they cover taste and appearance as well as safety. The regulations specify the maximum admissible concentrations for substances in drinking water, and for many of them also recommend guidance concentrations, which are often much lower. For example, the maximum admissible concentrations for aluminium and nitrates are 0·2 mg/l and 50 mg/l, whereas their respective guidance concentrations are 0·05 mg/l and 25 mg/l. Complying with these standards will cost about £3·8 billion up to the year 2000, and the water industry thinks that the interpretation of the requirements is too harsh. Mr Alan Neald from Thames Water pointed out that the European limits are based on safe concentrations for lifetime exposure to various substances. He also told me that Britain is not the only country having difficulty in implementing the directive—only two member countries have not been threatened with disciplinary action by the community. Given that the guidance levels are often much lower than the maximum admissible concentrations, however, the laws are unlikely to be relaxed.

About 70% of Britain's drinking water comes from rivers and the rest from underground sources. The National Rivers Authority is responsible for the use of water resources and enforces pollution control based on standards determined by the uses to which the water is put. The quality of water sources depends largely on pollution control. Over 80% of sewage discharged into rivers or tidal waters is treated biochemically first. Water authorities spent over £100 m in capital and operating costs in 1987 in collecting, treating, and disposing of sewage.

Because the quality of the supply varies so much there is no single set treatment for water, but figure 1 summarises the usual steps in water purification, although new techniques using ozone or activated charcoal are being developed. River water is held in raw storage tanks before processing. Sedimentation and some early purification occur here, but the main advantage is that if sources become polluted the intake to the reservoirs can be closed until the contaminated water has passed. (This often happens for a few days in autumn if the concentration of nitrate in river water rises when rain leaches out fertilisers used on farms in the summer.)

After purification water is disinfected before distribution. The

33

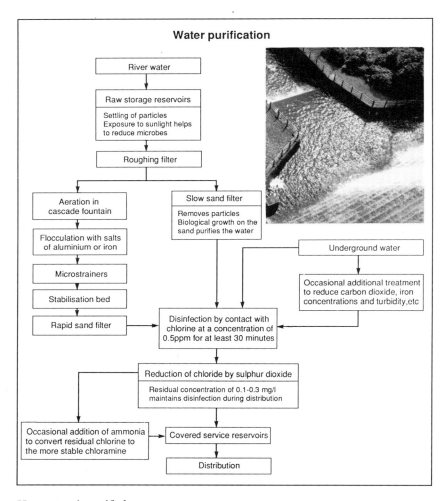

Water purification

River water

↓

Raw storage reservoirs

Settling of particles
Exposure to sunlight helps
to reduce microbes

↓

Roughing filter

Aeration in cascade fountain

↓

Flocculation with salts of aluminium or iron

↓

Microstrainers

↓

Stabilisation bed

↓

Rapid sand filter

Slow sand filter

Removes particles
Biological growth on the sand purifies the water

Underground water

Occasional additional treatment to reduce carbon dioxide, iron concentrations and turbidity, etc

Disinfection by contact with chlorine at a concentration of 0.5ppm for at least 30 minutes

↓

Reduction of chloride by sulphur dioxide

Residual concentration of 0.1-0.3 mg/l maintains disinfection during distribution

Occasional addition of ammonia to convert residual chlorine to the more stable chloramine

Covered service reservoirs

↓

Distribution

How water is purified

chlorination of drinking water is perhaps the single most important public health measure ever introduced. Most of the chlorine is removed before distribution, but a small amount is left to maintain disinfection during distribution.

Maintaining standards

Microbiological and chemical quality control tests are required at each stage of purification.[3] The new water companies are also responsible for quality throughout the distribution system and for maintaining the pipework as far as the stopcock in houses. The quality control checks include random tests for the plumbing metals: copper, lead, and zinc. In the past domestic plumbing has been identified as a source of lead in drinking water and the concentration has correlated with the blood concentration of lead in occupants.[4] Modern pipework is made of copper or plastic, but lead is still used in solders and there are many lead pipes left in Britain. In soft water regions like Scotland orthophosphate is often added to water to reduce its plumbisolvency. The current European standard for lead in drinking water is a maximum concentration of 50 µg/l, and achieving this throughout Britain is one of the major obstacles to meeting the new directive.

Recent legislation has established an independent drinking water inspectorate to monitor quality, but the office is not yet up and running. Since the privatisation of the industry was announced the water companies have been inundated with queries from the public about the quality of drinking water and how it is controlled. Although the water companies are required to make the results of their quality control tests available to the public, the regulations are so complicated and the results of tests so technical that it is unlikely that many people will be able to make much sense of them.

Responsibility for water quality does not stop with the supplying company—local authorities also have a duty to "make themselves aware" of the quality of water in their areas. This vague requirement is open to interpretation, but, as Graham Jukes from the Institution of Environmental Health Officers told me, local authorities could be criticised in the event of an incident if they have relied on the statistics produced by the industry, and they may also face criticism for spending large amounts of money on their own tests. Environmental health officers have always been responsible for making quality checks on the private water companies; now they must also monitor the new ones, and they are already overworked. Over 400 more officers are needed in Britain—a shortage of about 8%. With so much public concern, the lack of information that can be understood by the public, and recent "bad press" it is perhaps not surprising that there is now a growing trade in home water treatment systems, which are of dubious benefit.

Sewage disposal

Sewerage and sewage disposal were brought under the control of the water authorities by the Water Act 1973, and they account for about a third of the operating costs and half the capital expenditure of the industry. Nearly 6500 sewage treatment works exist in England and Wales and about 250 000 km of sewers. The main aim of sewage treatment is to remove the organic matter and decrease the biochemical demand for oxygen before sewage is discharged into rivers or the sea.[5] Sewage treatment generates about a million tonnes of dry sludge each year. About half of this is used on agricultural land where it is a useful source of nitrates and phosphates. The amount that can be used in agriculture, however, is limited by the concentrations of pathogenic microorganisms and toxic chemicals and the difficulties of transporting sewage sludge. Some sludge is used for landfill projects, and some is incinerated (although that is expensive). Figure 2 shows the main steps in sewage treatment.

Access to basic amenities

A national policy on water quality and sewage disposal is all very well, but it is of little benefit to families who do not have access to basic sanitary provision. In 1986, 463 000 houses in Britain still lacked one or more of the basic amenities of a kitchen sink, wash hand basin, shower or bath, and indoor toilet. In the private rented sector 8% of properties lacked at least one of these.[6] Many people live in multiple occupier houses in which, although the amenities may exist, access to them is limited. Access to facilities is important in determining health: studies of people rehoused from slums have shown that standards of hygiene rise when clean water is freely available, even without specific educational programmes.[7]

Health can be put at risk if sanitary equipment is not properly maintained or used. Flushing a toilet creates splashes and aerosols, which have the potential of spreading infection. The flushing

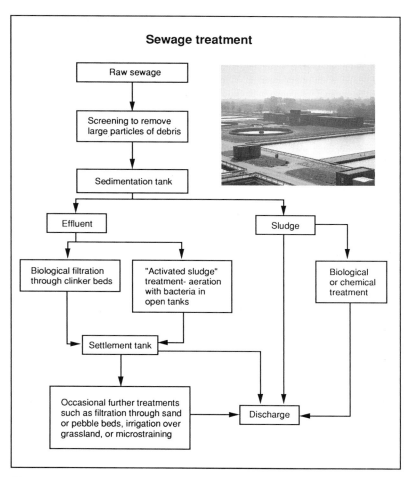

Sewage treatment

Raw sewage

↓

Screening to remove large particles of debris

↓

Sedimentation tank

Effluent

Sludge

Biological filtration through clinker beds

"Activated sludge" treatment- aeration with bacteria in open tanks

Biological or chemical treatment

Settlement tank

Occasional further treatments such as filtration through sand or pebble beds, irrigation over grassland, or microstraining

Discharge

How sewage is treated

handle on a toilet and inner handles on bathroom doors are potential sources of infection, so it is better to have a wash hand basin in the same room as the toilet. These risks present little problem in most homes, where standards of hygiene are high and extra care can be taken if a family member is ill, but in houses in multiple occupation the bathroom and kitchen facilities are often shared by many people, none of whom may take on the responsi-

Can the public be sure that our water will remain safe?

bility for cleaning, and diarrhoeal diseases can spread rapidly.[8] Most of us take high standards of sanitary provision for granted and forget that the lack of basic amenities or ignorance of simple principles of hygiene are still common causes of infectious illness.

Domestic waste

A worrying public health problem that has received publicity recently is the vast increase in sightings of rats in our towns. Rats are vectors for diseases including leptospirosis and can also inflict nasty bites. Surface infestations of rats have increased by a third in the past year in London and by as much as a half in some places. Many press reports have blamed the rise on poor maintenance of Britain's sewers.[9] A spokeswoman for Thames Water told me that, although the number of rats sighted above ground has increased, they have recorded no increase in the sightings of sewer rats. The Institution of Environmental Health Officers, however, emphasises that poor maintenance of sewers is an important factor in the increase in numbers of rats, along with increased demolition work, food waste, and tipping. It is planning a joint study with the Ministry of Agriculture, Fisheries, and Food to provide objective evidence about the problem.

Accumulation of rubbish has other health effects too. Broken

Rats are on the increase, but who is going to solve the problem?

glass is obviously dangerous, litter is a fire hazard, and the sight and smell of rotting debris is depressing. Each household in Britain produces, on average, over 11 kg of domestic refuse each week. Usually the local authority rubbish collection systems work well, but, particularly in blocks of flats where rubbish chutes or bins may be a long way from individual front doors, the system can break down. When it does there are too few environmental health officers and too little local government funding to ensure that things are put right.

Conclusions and comments

Most people in Britain have access to high quality water supplies and waste and sewage disposal services. Some of our most vulner-

39

able groups are, however, deprived of basic sanitary amenities or have only limited access to poorly maintained facilities. Poor hygiene is still a cause of infectious illness in Britain. Doctors still have a role in educating their patients about such matters and in campaigning for an end to the overcrowded unsanitary conditions that many families endure.

Although we now have laws to protect the quality of our drinking water, the recent privatisation of the industry has led to public concern that standards may be sacrificed to profit. Independent information about quality should be not only available to the public but also made understandable to lay people. People's fears will not be easily allayed by an understaffed inspectorate, and environmental health officers are already overworked. Public confidence and public health require that this is corrected.

1 World Health Organisation. *Guidelines for healthy housing*. Copenhagen: WHO, 1988.
2 McCarthy M. Britain facing legal action on water. *The Times* 1989; April 19.
3 Department of the Environment. *Water supply (water quality) regulations*. London: HMSO, 1989.
4 Goldberg A. Drinking water as a source of lead pollution. *Environmental Health Perspectives*. 1974 May:103–5.
5 Hall C. *Running water. The essential guide to the water services—how they work and the leisure facilities they provide*. London: Robertson McCarta, 1989.
6 Department of the Environment. *English house condition survey 1986*. London: HMSO, 1988.
7 Alvarez ML, Wurgaft F. Changes in hygienic habits in food preparation: facilities to use water. *Can J Public Health* 1987;**70**:43–6.
8 Conway J, eds. *Prescription for poor health. The health crisis for homeless families*. London: London Food Commission, Maternity Alliance, SMAC, Shelter, 1988.
9 Anonymous. Rat scandal. *Daily Hazard* 1988;**19**:1.

Noise, space, and light

It can be difficult to prove that any given aspect of housing is harmful to health. But often that is the wrong approach anyway. Houses should not be designed just to prevent harm to their occupants but also to promote health. This fact is well illustrated by three aspects of housing that affect wellbeing—noise, space, and light—but differ in the obviousness of their effects.

Noise

The structure of a building determines how well it transmits sound. Airpaths over or through party walls and unsealed pores in masonry transmit airborne sound. Ties in cavity walls can conduct sound, especially if mortar droppings are not cleaned off them during construction. Lightweight plastic ceilings on upper stories can cause reverberation in the roof space. Non-rigid layers attached to walls or floors can vibrate and reduce party wall insulation.

Though building regulations govern the transmission of sound between buildings, a recent study of newly completed but unoccupied houses gave poor results.[1] Over 1200 party walls and about 500 party floors were tested, and over half of the walls failed to meet the Building Research Establishment's recommended standard for the transmission of sound. The performance of a third of the floors was "very poor" for insulation of sounds caused by impact.

Noise is defined as unwanted sound. People are usually very tolerant of sounds they make themselves, but when they have no control over the source or if the sound is unwelcome it becomes noise. People vary in their ability to tolerate noise. Old people are often particularly sensitive, even at low intensities, probably

41

because their reduced hearing acuity makes them less able to select out particular sounds from the background noise. This then interferes with their ability to communicate effectively.[2]

Different types of noise cause different responses. In a recent review Mant and Gray concluded that traffic noise and impersonal sounds such as machines are often tolerated well.[3] One of the most irritating noises is human voices, and surprisingly the intensity of a sound is of little importance in determining the annoyance it causes.

In contrast to industrial exposure the problem of domestic noise is not one of a risk to hearing—although people who live with teenagers might doubt this. Hearing may be permanently damaged by regular exposure to noise of 75 dB for eight hours a day. Domestic appliances can generate high levels of sound—in one study the intensity of sound in a living room rose from a background of 50 dB to 81 dB during vacuuming[2]—but the exposure usually is so short that there is no risk to hearing.

The problem of domestic noise is one of annoyance. Most of us know the irritation of being woken up by a baby crying next door or the embarrassment of hearing neighbours rowing. For many people this is a constant problem and causes a great deal of stress. Apart from the effects of broken sleep and the sheer irritation of hearing other people's noise, there is the strain of knowing that neighbours can hear your noise too. This lack of privacy is often emphasised when people are asked to describe how their housing affects their wellbeing.[4][5]

It is difficult to provide hard data to prove that domestic noise causes serious distress, because many confounding variables operate. Modern houses with thin walls or slab block construction often transmit noise better than older, traditionally built houses. People living in tower blocks may be bombarded with noise from all sides, above, and below whereas those in detached houses will hear noise produced only by their own family—usually much less stressful. People living in poorly constructed houses or high rise flats differ from those in detached, traditionally built homes by a multitude of factors other than exposure to noise. It is difficult to prove that noise is causing stress when people are also coping with low incomes, overcrowding, cold damp homes, lifts that don't work, and so on.

No studies have yet produced firm evidence that domestic noise

*People living in tower blocks may be bombarded with
noise from all directions*

does serious harm,[3] but we should accept that it is a potential
source of irritation and can act in combination with other factors to
increase the stresses felt by many people living in modern housing.

Space

Descriptions of Victorian slums emphasise the overcrowding
and poor sanitation as causes of death and disease. In his study of

43

11 560 families from the "wage earning classes" in York in 1899 Rowntree found that a tenth of them were living more than two to a room.[6] (He compared that favourably with Glasgow, where over half the population was overcrowded.)

In Victorian slums the number of people sleeping in a room was a useful indicator of overcrowding. Today, when conditions are so much better, it is harder to decide what to measure. Should we look at floor area or room volume per person, or the number of people per available living room (excluding bathrooms and kitchens), or the number of bedrooms as a function of the number of adults of each sex in the household? The 1957 Housing Act contained a formula for calculating maximum acceptable occupancy of a dwelling based on the number of bedrooms and living rooms ("habitable rooms"). Children were allowed a half allowance, with no provision for infants. The annual reports of the registrar general define overcrowding as more than two people in each habitable room.

Given the emphasis on overcrowding in the past, there is surprisingly little evidence that it is still a major risk to health. Geographical and social class differences in mortality from some diseases have been ascribed to overcrowded living conditions in childhood.[7 8] If the number of people using a dwelling is separated from other variables such as poverty and social class, however, overcrowding is often found to have very little influence on health. This reflects the high quality of sanitation of most homes. The 1986 English house condition survey found that 139 000 homes still had no inside toilet and 151 000 had no hot water, but many of these properties were vacant and under repair.[9] Less than 1% of the population lives in such conditions, and even for most of them life is far removed from the shared privies, open sewers, and communal pumps of former slums.

But overcrowding still has a serious potential risk to health. We should not be too smug about our progress from the slums. "Houses in multiple occupation" cover a multitude of sins, including houses converted into flats, student lodgings, hostels, and the notorious bed and breakfast hotels for homeless families. The conditions in some of these are little better than in Victorian slums: many families have to share washing, toilet, food storage, and cooking facilities. In these properties infectious diseases, especially childhood diarrhoeas, are common.[10]

These very overcrowded conditions, with people living on top of each other and belongings stacked everywhere, also put inhabitants at risk of accidents, especially fire; and when accidents happen the escape routes are often inadequate to deal with the large number of people to be evacuated. In 1844 Engels could see the association between overcrowding and a high incidence of burns and scalds in children[11]—yet another lesson that we are now having to relearn. The Institution of Environmental Health Officers wants the law to be tightened to introduce national codes of practice and mandatory inspection and licensing of houses in multiple occupation to try to reduce these risks to health and safety.[12]

Nowadays overcrowding is usually seen more as a threat to mental than to physical health. One of the extreme examples of modern overcrowding is Hong Kong, where population densities can exceed 4000 an acre. A study of people living in Hong Kong found that the median allocation of space was as little as $4\,m^2$ (43 square feet) a person, with over a quarter of people sleeping more than three to a bed and almost two fifths sharing their home with non-related people.[13 14] After controlling for poverty, however, the study showed few major ill effects of this high density. Parents tended to allow their children to play outside unsupervised and people were unwilling to entertain at home, but mental health, family relationships, and performance at work did not seem to suffer. The only factor that was consistently associated with stress was the number of non-related households in each dwelling.

Mitchell has emphasised the difference between density (the number of people per unit space) and congestion (the number of simultaneous demands for the use of available space).[15] Mental health seems to be affected by overcrowding, but it is the lack of personal control over the available space rather than the small space available that seems to be important. This fits in with Newman's theories of the importance of "defensible space" (space under the resident's personal control).[16] Personal control over space, such as that gained from having a private front door approached through a defined garden, Newman says, engenders pride and security. Conversely, lack of control, as found in impersonal tower blocks with a single entry point set in communal grounds, creates hostility and promotes vandalism. Personal control over one's home environment does seem to be important.

In Hong Kong people live at densities of over 4000 an acre

Light

The health effects of domestic lighting are not immediately obvious. The latest review of the building regulations removed the requirement for window areas to be a set percentage of floor surface area, and there is now nothing in the regulations to prevent someone from building a house without windows.

When discussing the health effects of domestic lighting few think beyond photoepilepsy and the possibility that fluorescent lights can cause skin cancer. Some people certainly are sensitive to flicker from fluorescent tubes and television sets, but so few people are affected and the problem is so easily spotted and remedied that this is not a major risk to health.

Scare stories about the possibility that artificial light can induce skin cancer surface from time to time. In 1982 a study from Australia suggested that occupational exposure to fluorescent light was a risk factor for malignant melanoma.[17] But the lesions were distributed mainly on the trunk and this theory did not fit in well with other evidence about the carcinogenic effects of ultraviolet light. Dr Allister McKinlay from the National Radiological Protection Board emphasises that domestic exposure to fluorescent light is only intermittent, but in any case his studies of the emission spectra of commonly used domestic fluorescent tubes after 0, 100, and 2000 hours of use have not found any evidence that they are harmful.[18]

Dr McKinlay is much more concerned about the ultraviolet emission from tungsten halogen spotlights—now becoming fashionable as desk lamps. After they are used for a few hours the exposed skin on hands and forearms develops erythema. The amount of blue light emitted by the lamps is enough to cause retinal damage, but fortunately the lamps are so bright that most people cannot look at them for long. Perhaps the most worrying feature of these lamps is their operating temperature, about 300°C—a real hazard to users and inquisitive children.[19]

A new health effect of domestic light has emerged recently with descriptions of the seasonal affective disorder,[20] in which some people develop cyclical depression in the winter months with a return to normal in the spring. The mechanism is unknown, but day length is thought to be important. There is some evidence that exposure to bright light for several hours a day during winter will prevent this.[21] No particular wavelength seems to be needed so long as the light is bright.

The most important health problem to do with domestic lighting arises from the fact that nearly two thirds of British homes are inadequately lit. People struggling to do close work such as reading or sewing may suffer tension headaches and tire easily, but more worrying is the risk of accidents in badly lit kitchens or dim stairways. One survey in 1979–80 found that three quarters of homes had a single ceiling light, usually fitted with a 100 W bulb, as the only source of light in the kitchen.[22] There was a positive correlation between higher social class and more than one light source in the kitchen. None of the homes met the standard of an illumination level of 100 lux at the bottom of a flight of stairs recommended by the Chartered Institution of Building Services and the Illuminating Engineering Society. And the standards

Nearly two thirds of British homes are inadequately lit

suggested in their code are about 60% of the equivalent levels of light recommended in industry.

At least a quarter of a million people in Britain, most of them elderly, have substantially limited sight. The Partially Sighted Society is concerned that health workers rarely appreciate the benefits of good lighting, yet many doctors will have come across patients who complain of poor vision but perform well when tested in clinic. It is worth checking that the lighting in these people's homes is adequate.

A useful leaflet for people with visual impairment (and for the health workers who advise them) is produced by the Partially Sighted Society. It contains tips such as using strong contrasting colours to enhance visual clues, choosing wide lightshades that reflect as much light as possible, and carefully shielding lamps to avoid glare—particularly disabling for people with cataracts—while not reducing too much the amount of light transmitted.[24]

Often the amount of illumination can be increased very easily at little expense to the patient. A fluorescent tube gives better illumination at lower cost than an ordinary light bulb but may not be so aesthetically pleasing. A dirty net curtain may block up to 85% of daylight entering a room, though a clean one will allow up to 70% of the light through. As much as half of the illumination from a single ceiling light is obtained after reflection from the walls, ceiling, and floor, so the choice of colour schemes for internal decorations can affect the illumination in a room greatly.[23]

Conclusions

Domestic noise poses no great risk to physical health but may be an important source of irritation and stress. Overcrowding can endanger physical health if the demands on the sanitary services to a property are high or if there are inadequate means of detecting and escaping from a fire. Domestic lighting has a surprisingly large effect on physical health because so few homes are adequately lit to ensure the safety of occupants, especially the elderly. Poor domestic lighting may also influence mental health, although this is an unresearched subject.

49

Comment

The effects of noise, space, and light on the wellbeing of occupants show how complicated the analysis of housing and health can be. In industry noise intensity has a clear association with physical health, but industrial standards are not always applicable to domestic settings.

History has taught us that overcrowding can endanger health, but recent studies have found only subtle effects of congestion on mental health, and overcrowding has been rather played down. In many hostels and hotels we are now having to relearn the lessons of the Victorian slums. The basic principles of housing and health do not change much, and we ignore them at our peril.

Domestic lighting might not at first be expected to have much effect on physical health, but its potential to contribute to accidents, especially in elderly people, is shocking and underestimated. Housing often influences health indirectly, but we seldom look carefully enough for the association.

1   Sewell EC, Scholes WE. *Sound insulation performance between dwellings built in the early 1970s*. Garston: Department of the Environment (Building Research Establishment), 1978.

2   Farr LE. Medical consequences of environmental home noises. *JAMA* 1967;**202**:171–4.

3   Mant DC, Gray JAM. *Building regulations and health*. Garston: Department of the Environment (Building Research Establishment), 1986.

4   Cappon D. Mental health in the high-rise. *Can J Public Health* 1971;**62**:426–31.

5   Duvall D, Booth A. The housing environment and women's health. *J. Health Soc Behav* 1978;**19**:410–7.

6   Rowntree BS. *Poverty. A study of town life*. London: Nelson, 1901.

7   Barker DJP, Osmond C. Inequalities in health in Britain: specific explanations in three Lancashire towns. *Br Med J* 1987;**294**:749–52.

8   Barker DJP, Coggon D, Osmond C, Wickham C. Poor housing in childhood and high rates of stomach cancer in England and Wales. *Br J Cancer* 1990;**61**:575–8.

9   Department of the Environment. *English house condition survey 1986*. London: HMSO, 1988.

10 Conway J, ed. *Prescription for poor health. The health crisis for homeless families*. London: London Food Commission, Maternity Alliance, SHAC, Shelter, 1988.

11 Engels F. *Condition of the working class in England in 1844*. London: George Allen and Unwin, 1892.

12 Institution of Environmental Health Officers. *Houses in multiple occupation*. London: IEHO, 1984.

13 Mitchell RE. Some social implications of high density housing. *American Sociological Review* 1971;**36**:18–29.

14 Mitchell RE. Misconceptions about manmade space: in partial defense of high density housing. *The Family Coordinator* 1974; January:51–6.
15 Mitchell RE. Cultural and health influences on building, housing, and community standards: cost implications for the human habitat. *Human Ecology* 1976;4:297–330.
16 Newman D. *Defensible space: crime prevention through urban design*. New York: Macmillan, 1972.
17 Beral V, Evans S, Shaw H, Milton G. Malignant melanoma and exposure to fluorescent lighting at work. *Lancet* 1982;**ii**:290–3.
18 Whillock M, Clark IE, McKinlay AF, Todd CD, Mundy EJ. *Ultraviolet radiation levels associated with the use of fluorescent general lighting. UV-A and UV-B lamps in the workplace and home*. Chilton: National Radiological Protection Board, 1988.
19 McKinlay AF, Whillock MJ, Meulemans CCE. *Ultraviolet radiation and blue light emissions from spotlights incorporating tungsten halogen lamps*. Chilton: National Radiological Protection Board, 1989.
20 Rosenthal NE, Sack DA, Carpenter CJ, Parry BL, Mendelson WB, Wehr TA. Antidepressant effects of light in seasonal affective disorder. *Am J Psychiatry* 1985;**142**:163–9.
21 Rosenthal NE, Skwerer RG, Jacobsen FM, Hardin TA, Wehr TA. Phototherapy: the NIMH experience. In: Thompson C, Silverstone T, eds. *Seasonal affective disorder*. London: CNS Publishers, 1989.
22 Simpson J, Tarrant AWS. A study of lighting in the home. In: Swinburne H, ed. *Lighting research technology*. London: Chartered Institution of Building Services, 1983 (Vol 15, No 1).
23 Jay P. Fundamentals. In: Greenhalgh R. *Light for low vision*. Hove: Partially Sighted Society, 1980;13–29. (Proceedings of symposium held at University College London, 1978.)
24 Electricity Council, Partially Sighted Society. *Lighting and low vision*. London: Electricity Council, Partially Sighted Society, 1981.

Electromagnetic radiation in homes

Probably the greatest risk to health from electricity is electrocution or fire caused by incorrectly installed or maintained equipment,[1] but in this chapter I will discuss the less obvious problem of exposure to electric and magnetic fields. Many people have a vague worry that living near distribution pylons or cables may be bad for them, but is there any firm evidence of this?

Electromagnetic fields can induce eddy currents in biological tissues. Any object that has an electric charge has an electric field around it, the strength of which is expressed as volts per metre. In

Do pylons and cables near homes pose a threat to health?

Britain the highest voltage overhead cables carry 400 kV, and at ground level directly below them an electric field of about 10 kV/m is possible. The fields generated by these high voltage lines have a range of 200–300 metres if unshielded, but for local low voltage distribution lines the range is only 10–20 metres.

The worry that exposure to strong electric fields might damage health was raised in the late 1960s and early 1970s by reports that Russian workers in 500 and 750 kV substations were complaining of vague symptoms including headaches, lethargy, and loss of libido (V P Korobhova, Conference Internationale des Grandes Réseaux Electrique à Haute Tension, Paris, 1972). The Russians concluded that the symptoms were a stress response to frequent microshocks from touching conducting objects in the strong fields. But a laboratory study of the effects of induced electric currents found no association with stress (J A Bonnell et al, conference on electric and magnetic fields in medicine, London, 1985).

Some possible explanations for these symptoms came from a study in electricity workers in Britain.[2] They used personal dosimeters to record their exposure to electric fields and were questioned about their health by interviewers who were blind to the results of the exposure studies. There was no significant correlation between exposure and health, but there was an association between poor health and working alone, working long hours, and recent changes in shift patterns.

It is impossible to tell from the Russian studies whether such factors might have influenced their results. Even if the electric fields were to blame they must have been extremely large. In houses we are exposed to the electric fields generated by electrical equipment and wiring, but these decrease rapidly with distance from the source and, like all electric fields, are easily shielded by objects in their way. It seems unlikely that the low electric field strengths found inside houses could damage health, but there are no hard data.

In 1989 the *Sunday Mirror* claimed that cot deaths were attributable to strong electric fields in the home. The story was taken up by the Channel 4 programme *Hard News*, which questioned the sensitivity of the dosimeter used and claimed that some of the interviews with bereaved parents had been misrepresented. The Foundation for the Study of Sudden Infant Deaths told *Hard News* that the articles had "caused almost a panic," but Brian

Maddock of the Central Electricity Research Laboratories told me that the evidence in the *Sunday Mirror* articles was so flimsy that his unit had not even considered investigating the possibility of an association.

Magnetic fields

A magnetic field is induced when electric current flows, its strength being measured in tesla (1 microtesla = 1 ampere per metre). One American study reported magnetic fields of 1000–

We rely on electricity for many home comforts, but are they doing us any harm?

54

2000 microT a few centimetres from hand held electrical objects such as hairdriers and shavers, but the field strength fell rapidly with distance from the object and was negligible about a metre from the source.[3] The magnetic fields associated with the highest voltage overhead cables in Britain are up to 100 microT. If ill effects of electromagnetic radiation in homes are experienced they are probably caused by exposure to magnetic fields: typically these are better inducers of eddy currents than are ordinary electric fields. Unlike electric fields, magnetic fields are hard to shield and readily penetrate materials, including the body. Trees and houses do not shield us from the magnetic fields generated by power distribution lines near our homes, and one worry is that there may be harmful effects from exposure to these fields.

Attention has focused on the possible non-thermal effects of electromagnetic radiation on human health. Data from animal and cell studies support the existence of such effects,[4] but it is important to distinguish between the observation of a biological effect and proof that it does any harm.

Cables and cancer

Claims that electromagnetic radiation does harm human health are common. In Britain Perry *et al* found significantly stronger magnetic fields outside the homes of people who had committed suicide than those of controls,[5] and the various claims of harmful effects of electromagnetic radiation have been summarised.[6] One of the most worrying claims is the suggestion that exposure to strong electromagnetic fields may increase the risk of childhood cancers. In 1977 Wertheimer and Leeper in Denver, Colorado, compared the home environments of children with cancer with those of controls and suggested that there was an association between cancer and the density of power lines carrying high current loads near the children's homes.[7] They based their assessment on a coding system for the lines rather than on direct measurement of the fields in the homes. The line configuration was coded by people who were aware of the case or control status of the children in the house, and there were no controls for housing density or industrial pollution.

A case control study in Yorkshire that used information from electricity board records to calculate magnetic fields in children's homes found no significantly increased risk of childhood cancer with increasing field strength (A Myers *et al*, conference on electric and magnetic fields in medicine and biology, London 1985). But no data were available about past exposure, and again no direct measurements were made of the fields.

In 1986, as part of the New York State Power Lines Project, Savitz and colleagues studied childhood cancers and magnetic fields in homes.[8] Like Wertheimer and Leeper they used codes based on the configuration of high current lines, but the people coding the houses were blind to the children's health, and point measurements of magnetic fields in the homes were also made. Savitz and his colleagues found a small significant association between cancer and a high current configuration of power lines, but a much weaker association with measured fields (figure).

So the configuration of the wiring is possibly a better guide to chronic exposure to magnetic fields than are point measurements. Even so, another explanation is that some other factor, such as overcrowding or pollution, is operating. Even Savitz was cautious about the implications of his research: "our study is not sufficiently convincing to warrant drastic action by homeowners."

Exposure to electromagnetic fields in houses depends on three factors: the type of nearby power lines; the current flowing in them; and the distance of the house from the lines. Buildings offer little shielding from magnetic fields, and there is no easy way to reduce domestic exposure. Brian Maddock thinks that no ill effects of electromagnetic fields in houses have been proved conclusively but that enough questions have been raised to warrant further investigation. He is particularly concerned that publication bias might have suppressed studies that had negative results, and he also doubts whether the public is able to interpret preliminary scientific reports fairly. The Central Electricity Generating Board is studying the magnetic climate across Britain using mobile monitoring vans. It is also studying individual exposure using personal dosimeters, and is planning national studies of domestic exposure to electromagnetic fields and the risk of childhood leukaemia.

Conclusion

No firm evidence exists that domestic exposure to electromagnetic fields harms health. On the other hand, neither is there any

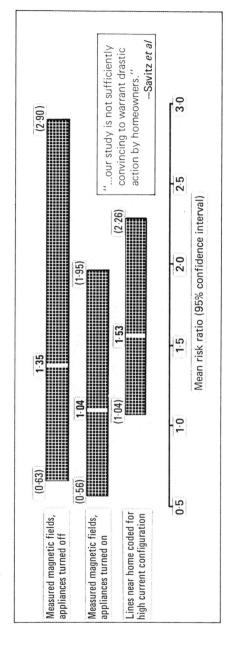

Childhood cancer and magnetic fields due to power lines[5]

good evidence to calm public fears generated by scare stories in the press.

Comment

We urgently need high quality epidemiological studies into the effects, if any, of electromagnetic fields on human health. We do not even know what to study—should we look at maximum field strengths; changes in field strengths; average exposure; electric or magnetic fields, or both; induced currents; or something quite separate? If the figures of Savitz *et al* are correct then domestic exposure to electromagnetic fields might double the incidence of childhood cancers. This would still produce only about two cases per 10 000 a year, although this is two too many. Any study that aims at providing useful information must therefore be very carefully designed and performed. When the electricity industry in Britain is privatised the National Grid Company is destined to take over the Central Electricity Generating Board's studies. These investigations must not be lost in the process of reorganisation.

1 Stockting J. The safety of house wiring installations. In: Institution of Environmental Health Officers. *Homes safety and the environment*. London: IEHO, 1987.
2 Broadbent DE, Broadbent MHP, Male JC, Jones MRL. Health of workers exposed to electric fields. *Br J Indust Med* 1985;**42**:75–84.
3 Deadman JE, Camus M, Armstrong BG, *et al*. Occupational and residential 60-Hz electromagnetic fields and high frequency electric transients: exposure assessment using a new dosimeter. *Am Ind Hyg Assoc J* 1988;**49**:409–19.
4 National Radiological Protection Board. *Guidance as to restrictions on exposures to time varying electromagnetic fields and the 1988 recommendations of the International Non-Ionising Radiation Committee*. Didcot: NRPB, 1989.
5 Perry FS, Reichmanis M, Marino A, Becker RO. Environmental power-frequency magnetic fields and suicide. *Health Physics* 1981;**4**:267–77.
6 Best S. Killing fields: epidemiological evidence. *Electronics World and Wireless World* 1990; February:98–106.
7 Wertheimer N, Leeper E. Electrical wiring configuration and childhood cancer. *Am J Epidemiol* 1979;**109**:273–84.
8 Savitz DA, Wachtel H, Barnes FA, John EM, Tvrdik JG. Case-control study of childhood cancer and exposure to 60-Hz magnetic fields. *Am J Epidemiol* 1988;**128**:21–38.

Accidents at home

Every year about 5500 fatal accidents occur in British homes (some two fifths of all fatal accidents). A further 2·2 million people have non-fatal accidents at home needing hospital treatment, and another 900 000 are dealt with by general practitioners. The cost of domestic accidents to the health service in England and Wales is about £300 million a year.[1]

Statistical information about non-fatal domestic accidents has been collected since 1976 by the Department of Trade and Industry, based on attendance records at the accident departments of 20 hospitals. Information about fatal accidents is held in the home accident deaths database, and the Home Office publishes annual statistics related to fire.

Accidents and children

Accidents are the commonest cause of death in children aged over 1 year and account for a third of all childhood deaths. About three quarters of a million children are injured at home each year, and domestic accidents account for most of the falls, burns, and poisonings. Nevertheless, many of these accidents are preventable.[2] The accidents that happen to children often reflect their stage of development, which makes the accidents more predictable by adults. Under the age of 3 months one of the commonest accidents is being dropped by an adult; by 10 months children are crawling and starting to walk and risk hurting themselves on the sharp edges of furniture. Later, increasing independence brings risks from any hazard within their reach; falling from windows that open too far, swallowing household chemicals, and playing with matches. By school age, road traffic accidents have become important.

710 People died and 9480 were injured in house fires in 1987

From the age of 2 boys are about twice as likely to have an accident as girls. And childhood accidents also show a definite variation with social class,[3] this gradient being steeper than for any other cause of death in children. Thus in Haringey, London, in one year nearly a fifth of children under 5 attended an accident and emergency department, three quarters of them because of an accident at home (P Constantinides and G Walker, unpublished data). Children from the least affluent parts of the borough were four times more likely to have an accident than those from the most affluent parts, and there was a significant association between accident rates and unemployment, overcrowding, rented tenure, poor parental education, and low social class.

Elderly people are also at risk of accidents at home. As with children, their risk is influenced by what they can or cannot do. Deteriorating sight and poor mobility may put them at risk of falls; open or portable fires rather than central heating are a fire hazard; and frailty or lack of money may prevent them from maintaining equipment properly. In 1987, 18% of people who died in fires were aged 60–74, and a quarter were over 75.[4]

The guidelines about designing safer houses produced by the Child Accident Prevention Trust are based on studies of the type and incidence of accidents to children at home.[5] Many of the guidelines also apply to other groups at risk, including the elderly. Some of the recommendations—L shaped flights of stairs to reduce the distance in a fall, no doors or windows opening on to stairways, and through routes in kitchens that avoid the cooker— are best introduced during planning. Others can be incorporated easily into existing homes: good lighting of stairwells, handrails with an all round grab, no cupboards above the cooker, non-slip floor surfaces in kitchens, safety glazing for shower screens, and so on. If all of the recommended features were incorporated into the design of a new house the trust estimates that the total cost would be increased by only 5%.

Rules and regulations

Because the cause of so many domestic accidents is predictable it is possible to legislate for safety standards that reduce the risks— for example, restrictions on the flammability of children's nightwear and on how far windows in multistorey dwellings may open.[6]

One important problem that has not been properly dealt with so far is domestic architectural glass, which was found to cause no less than half the injuries seen in a group of 80 children with lacerations.[7] Ten years ago the author of that report concluded that safety glass should be used in all glass doors, French windows, patio doors, and the lower parts of windows—but our hospitals are still treating over 400 000 such injuries every year (R Sinnott, conference of Institution of Environmental Health Officers, London, 1987). Nearly half are associated with glass in doors, and two fifths of them happen to children under 15.

There are regulations covering the use of glass in buildings. British Standard code of practice BS 6262 specifies that safety glass must be used in fully glazed doors. The code defines a fully glazed door as being one in which the glazed panel is at least 300 mm wide and comes within 150 mm of the edges and top of the door and within 300 mm of the bottom. Any other type of door is not covered by the code. The code also specifies that safety glass should be used in windows less than 800 mm from the floor in places where many people move about. The concept of "many people" is vague, and would not apply in most homes. Many homes contain large areas of glass that would not be covered by the code and present a real danger, especially to children and elderly people.

The regulations covering safety glass are also confusing. British Standard 6206 covers the impact performance of flat safety glass and safety plastics and divides them into three classes: A, B, and C. Class C is the minimum acceptable standard for low level glazing and B that for doors and side panels. Plastics are often safer than glass, but they tend to bow and discolour with time and are easily scratched. "Wired glass" is not necessarily safe. The mesh holds the shattered pieces of glass together, but does not increase the strength of the glass under impact. "Laminated glass" consists of two layers of annealed glass with an interleaved and bonded layer of plastic. It is just as likely to crack as any other annealed glass, but the plastic layer holds the pieces together. Laminated glass may be of safety class A, but this should not be assumed. People wanting safe glass for domestic use should use "toughened glass." This has a high compressive strength, and because it tends to break into small cuboid pieces it is always safety class A, regardless of its thickness.

The restricted applications of regulations about domestic glass and the confusing range of products available make it hard for householders to know whether their homes are safe or not, and perhaps it would be better to stipulate that the highest grade of safety glass should be used for all domestic glazing.

Safe as houses? How safe is safety glass?

Limitations of legislation

Laws to improve home safety have drawbacks as well as advantages. The standards may not be hard and fast enough—indeed, the present standards for safety glass are under review after recent publicity about the death of a boy whose heart was punctured by a spear of glass from a conservatory fitted with toughened glass that met current standards. Other factors may need to be considered—for example, is the best safety glass easy to break if it is necessary to escape from a fire? There is also the question of personal freedom, given that most people regard their homes as places where they can do as they like. Many home safety features are therefore couched as recommendations, rather than laws.

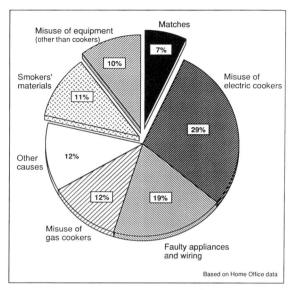

Causes of accidental fires in dwellings in 1987

Laws and recommendations may be combined, as in the case of domestic wiring. For new houses the local electricity board must be satisfied with the standard of wiring before connecting the supply; thereafter things are left to the owner's discretion. Fixed wiring should last for 20 to 30 years if properly used, although of course systems installed 20 years ago were not designed to cope with the proliferation of electrical domestic equipment that has occurred since. Sockets, switches, and circuit breakers are subject to mechanical wear and have a shorter life.

Ideally, domestic wiring should be checked every five years. In 1986 a total of 47 electrocutions occurred in the home (J Stockting, conference of Institution of Environmental Health Officers, London, 1987), and faulty electrical equipment and wiring are also common causes of domestic fires (figure). In 1987 there were 63 000 domestic fires in the United Kingdom,[4] and though they accounted for less than a fifth of all fires they accounted for no less than three quarters of all deaths and non-fatal injuries from this cause. Death occurs most commonly from the effects of gas and smoke; hence the installation of smoke detectors might have an important preventive role.

The incidence of domestic fires is significantly associated with unemployment, low socioeconomic status, and inversely with owner occupation.[8] Very overcrowded conditions increase the risk of fire and the difficulties of escaping from it. The Institution of Environmental Health Officers is particularly concerned about the risks in houses in multiple occupation.[9] The shortage of environmental health officers means that they are confined to reacting to complaints, rather than being able to inspect regularly. Until the service is adequately funded, the poorest and most disadvantaged members of our society will not be adequately protected from the dangers of badly maintained properties.

Prevention by education

Clearly, voluntary compliance with advice must remain the principal means of preventing accidents at home. Reinforcing such advice is, nevertheless, essential. A study in Newcastle on the effects of a national television campaign about childhood accidents found that over half of families with young children had seen none of the programmes, and only a tenth of those specifically encouraged to watch had taken any action as a result.[10] But almost two thirds of those families who had received specific advice at a home visit had taken action to improve domestic safety.

Thus people respond best to simple, specific advice directly relevant to their own homes when it is given separately from other information. It may not be possible to make special visits to all patients to advise on home safety, but doctors are well placed to give opportune advice during home visits or when a patient presents as the result of an accident.

Conclusion

Accidents at home place a heavy strain on health service resources, yet many domestic accidents are predictable and potentially preventable. Safety features can be incorporated into most houses fairly cheaply. Doctors are often ideally placed to offer advice not only about home safety, but also about what help is available from social security offices to provide families on low incomes with safety features like fireguards and stair gates. Legislation is no guarantee of domestic safety, but it at least provides some protection for the most vulnerable members of society. This protection is lost if the regulations cannot be enforced, and the present shortage of environmental health officers adds to the dangers.

1 Department of Trade and Industry. *Home and leisure accident research. Eleventh annual report home accident surveillance system: 1987 data*. London: DTI, 1989.
2 Child Accident Prevention Trust. *Basic principles of child accident prevention. A guide to action*. London: CAPT, 1989.
3 Constantinides P. Safe at home? Children's accidents and inequality. *Radical Community Medicine* 1988; Spring: 31–4.
4 Home Office. *Fire statistics United Kingdom 1987*. London: Government Statistical Service, 1989.
5 Page M. *Child safety and housing. Practical design guidelines for commissioning agencies, architects, designers, and builders*. London: Child Accident Prevention Trust, 1986.
6 Gloag D. *Colloquium on strategies for accident prevention. A review of the present position*. London: Medical Commission on Accident Prevention, 1987.
7 Jackson RH. Lacerations from glass in childhood. *Br Med J* 1981;**283**:1310–2.
8 Chandler SE, Chapman A, Hollington SJ. Fire incidence, housing and social conditions—the urban situation in Britain. *Fire Prevention* 1984;**172**:15–20.
9 Institution of Environmental Health Officers. *Houses in multiple occupation*. London: IEHO, 1984.
10 Colver AF, Hutchinson PJ, Judson EC. Promoting children's home safety. *Br Med J* 1982;**285**:1177–80.

Families and flats

No other housing system in Britain has such a bad reputation as flats. High rise, tower block, slab block, and even low rise are used as terms of abuse. Blocks of flats began to dominate the skyline in the 1960s in response to a great demand for new housing and the development of new, often untested, building techniques that offered the promise of quickly producing high density, low cost housing. Many of those blocks are now run down, ugly, and vandalised, and they have gained a reputation for being unhealthy. Do they really deserve this image?

Poor structure and design

I do not want to promote the popular myth that flats are inevitably bad places to live. The tallest flats in Britain—at the Barbican in London—are much sought after and very expensive. In many parts of Europe people live happily in blocks of flats. Chris Gossop from the Town and Country Planning Association emphasises, however, that there is a longer history of flat dwelling in Continental Europe, and the tradition of efficient concierges is important in maintaining repair and a sense of identity and security. It is rare to find good caretaking services in blocks of council flats in Britain, but this would help to alleviate many of the problems inherent in high rise living.

Assembling concrete slabs may have been quick, but poorly constructed joints let water in. Adding calcium chloride or using high alumina compounds were two measures used to speed the drying time of concrete; both are now banned because of the poor structural quality of the resulting product. When the concrete cracked, water penetrated and corroded the metal structural supports. Asbestos was widely used for insulating walls and pipes and has become exposed as the structure of many of these buildings has deteriorated; removing it is a serious problem.[1] Concrete has a high thermal mass, which made many of the buildings hard to heat, and this was compounded by cold bridging from supporting beams. Many blocks were fitted with electrical central heating systems that were cheap to install but are now expensive to run. Ill fitting, mass produced doors and windows encouraged draughts.

The building techniques meant that many flats were cold and damp—with all the known consequences for respiratory and cardiovascular health.[2] But many of the designs were also unhealthy. Perhaps the most obvious worry is safety. Windows and balconies present a great hazard to young children. Although locks and catches can be fitted to prevent windows opening too far, many children are injured each year in falls, and the dangers rise with height above the ground.

Maintenance in publicly owned buildings in Britain is notoriously bad, and poor maintenance in flats adds to the problems. When lifts are not adequately maintained people are forced to use the stairs. Vandalism in blocks of flats is also common, and if broken lights on stairwells are not repaired elderly people face an extra hazard on top of a long, steep climb. In the event of a fire, escape from a block of flats can be difficult, especially for the infirm and people with children. Stairwells and hallways in flats are usually invisible from nearby roads and houses and are ideal places for violent crime. The possibility of an attack is a common worry, especially for old people and women.

Children living in flats often have few opportunities for normal play. Although many blocks are surrounded by large expanses of grass, games are often forbidden. Even if there is somewhere to play it is seldom enclosed. Children are not adequately protected from passing traffic, dogs, or strangers; and their mothers may be several floors up—too far away to be able to keep an eye on them, much less to reach them quickly if trouble arises. Most mothers prefer to keep their children indoors rather than take such risks. Architects now accept that it is possible to achieve high density housing by careful design of two storey houses with individual gardens. The grassed areas around many blocks of flats are rarely used and are nothing more than a waste of space.

Defensible space

Fanning studied the health of British service families living in Germany and compared those allocated to flats with those placed in houses.[3] All of the families studied were of similar social class and had identical access to social and medical facilities, yet those living in flats showed half as much morbidity again as those in houses. In particular, respiratory illnesses were much more common in children living in flats, and Fanning concluded that this was because they were not allowed to play outside as much as those living in houses.

Another common hazard in poorly maintained blocks of flats is the accumulation of rubbish, with all the attendant risks of infections, fire, and other accidents. Often this is simply the result of bad planning—too few rubbish collection points too widely spaced; but there is the added problem that large parts of many blocks of flats are public areas, so no one feels any pride or responsibility for their upkeep. Litter and vandalism are especially common in the public parts of flats—the stairwells, lifts, entrances, garages, and surrounding grounds. Newman's theory of defensible

Where's the sense of pride or responsibility?

69

space helps to explain this.[4] Residents do not have any control over these public areas and so have no desire to maintain them. This contrasts with houses and gardens where responsibility is obvious and people "defend" their territory.

People living in high rise blocks feel isolated.[5] There is no sense of community, and young mothers in particular have no easy access to support from friends and neighbours. Getting out for a few hours is a difficult undertaking if you have to negotiate a pram and toddler down seemingly endless flights of stairs because the lift is broken. A survey in Glasgow found that people living in flats had a higher prevalence of mental symptoms than those in houses, and the effect increased with the number of floors.[6] In the service families studied by Fanning, women in their 20s were nearly three

Getting out for a few hours is a difficult undertaking

times as likely to present to their general practitioners with psychoneurotic problems if they lived in flats, even though none of the blocks was more than four storeys high.[3]

Of course, many of the problems faced by people living in modern housing estates are not confined to flat dwellers. When the large new estates were built the families who moved in often lost their previous supporting networks of family and friends. One study that found an unexpectedly high incidence of psychological disorder in residents of a new housing estate in Hertfordshire also reported a tendency for a gradual improvement with time as people settled in.[7] Recent work in London, Glasgow, and Edinburgh has confirmed that women have an increased risk of psychiatric disease, especially depression, if they live in damp houses, have very low incomes, are unemployed, or are bringing up children single handed (S D Platt *et al*, fifth European symposium on social psychiatry, Manchester, April 1989). Houses are more popular than flats, and there is a tendency for the more eloquent and capable council tenants to campaign successfully for a house. Those left in the flats are already a disadvantaged group, and the isolation and inconveniences of high rise living add to their problems.

Designing out problems

In recent years it has been fashionable to talk about designing out problems in estates. The patron of this concept is Alice Coleman, who produced a "disadvantagement score" based on her observations in several run down estates.[8] She assigned an acceptable threshold value for each of 15 design variables, and suggested that blocks of dwellings could be classified depending on how many thresholds were exceeded (table). This produced a score from 0 to 15, which she claimed correlated with vandalism, litter, graffiti, and even with the number of children in the block who were in care. A study in Thamesmead in south east London found that women tended to be more depressed if they lived in blocks classified as disadvantaged by Coleman's criteria.[9] Coleman makes strong claims about the causes of vandalism (box)—yet the absence of shops, schools, and play areas has been identified as a major contribution to problems in new housing estates.[10]

TABLE—*Threshold values for 15 design variables used to calculate Coleman's disadvantagement score*

Design variable	Threshold value
Overhead walkways	0
Stilts or garages	0
Play areas	0
Blocks per site	1
Existing interconnections	1
Vertical access routes	1
Storeys per dwelling	1
Storeys per block	3
Access points	1
Dwellings per corridor	4
Dwellings per entrance	6
Dwellings per block	12
Entrance type	Communal only
Entrance position	Facing the street
Spacial organisation	Single block or semi-public multi-block

Coleman has suggested that estates could be improved by modifying the blocks of flats to reduce their disadvantagement scores. She also suggests that new blocks should be designed to minimise their scores. But she seems to have confused correlation with cause. Her ideas are simplistic rather than simple—the variables are analysed on an all or none basis, with no allowance for the fact that bigger blocks house more people and might be expected to produce more graffiti, litter, and children in care.[11] In some places where estates have been modified in line with Coleman's ideas the results have been unpopular and crime rates have risen.[12] On the Mozart estate, in Southwark, London, overhead walkways were removed in line with Coleman's theories, but they had provided a convenient link between two parts of the estate on opposite sides of a road, and their removal isolated residents from their neighbours even more.

"Unemployment is not associated with increased vandalism. More residential green space brings more intensive abuse, and so does the presence of shops, services, or community halls located inside the estate."—Alice Coleman

Conclusions and comment

Perhaps in an ideal world all families would live in cosy semis with neat gardens, but in reality many families would be glad of a flat, even in a high rise block. Indeed, some people positively welcome the privacy that high rise living affords. Elderly people might find that living in a flat releases them from the maintenance of a home and garden—so long as the lifts work and proper security is provided.

Blocks of flats do not make ideal homes for families with young children. The way in which many of them were built creates hazards that are known to damage health. In addition, their design often creates problems of safety and isolation. Many of these difficulties could be corrected or prevented by providing adequate support services for people living in flats, but there is no simple solution that will turn problem flats into desirable residences overnight. New building programmes should avoid high rise blocks.

1 People's Asbestos Action Campaign. *Asbestos fact pack.* 3rd ed. London: PAAC, 1987.
2 Lowry S. Temperature and humidity. *Br Med J* 1989;**299**:1326–8.
3 Fanning DM. Families in flats. *Br Med J* 1967;**iv**:382–6.
4 Newman O. *Defensible space: crime prevention through urban design.* New York: Macmillan, 1972.
5 Richman N. The effects of housing on preschool children and their mothers. *Develop Med Child Neurol* 1974;**16**:53–8.
6 Hannay DR. Mental health and high flats. *J Chronic Dis* 1981;**34**:431–2.
7 Martin FM, Brotherston JHF, Chave SPW. Incidence of neurosis in a new housing estate. *Br J Prev Soc Med* 1957;**11**:196–202.
8 Coleman A. *Utopia on trial. Vision and reality in planned housing.* London: Hilary Shipman, 1985.
9 Birtchnell J, Masters N, Deahl M. Depression and the physical environment. A study of young married women on a London housing estate. *Br J Psychiatry* 1988;**153**:56–64.
10 Goodman M. The enclosed environment. *J R Soc Health* 1974;**94**:165–9.
11 Hillier B. City of Alice's dreams. *Architects Journal* 1986;**9** July:39–41.
12 Hillier B. Suburban Messiah. *Roof* 1988;March and April:42–3.

Housing for people with special needs

Britain has a long tradition of providing special housing for the elderly, and more recently the needs of the physically and mentally ill have been considered too. But are people with special housing needs being identified and properly catered for? And what can doctors do to help?

The elderly

There is no magical age at which one becomes "old," and any special housing needs are never a consequence of age alone but rather of accompanying financial, mental, or physical disability. The old include some of our poorest, most vulnerable citizens—in 1986 a fifth of single pensioners lived in houses needing more than £1000 worth of urgent repairs to the external fabric.[1] But there is also a growing group of affluent elderly consumers who can afford—and expect—the highest standards from their housing. As the proportion of old people in Britain rises they are becoming an increasingly influential political force and are more likely to succeed in changing public policy than many other groups with special housing needs.

Although aging is not a disease, older people are more likely to experience ill health than others and are less able to cope with the results. Old people are also particularly susceptible to any harmful effects of their housing. Housing for old people should be designed to prevent the more common problems.

Temperature

Hypothermia is probably the most widely recognised problem of housing for the elderly. Old people are especially vulnerable

74

Age and disability are not the same thing

because often they have reduced sensitivity to cold and impaired thermoregulation and because reduced mobility may hinder their ability to generate heat. The British Geriatrics Society advises old people to maintain their living rooms at 21°C, but in a national survey about half the old people had a living room temperature below 16°C, and a third had bedrooms colder than 10°C.[2]

Many old people cannot afford to heat their homes adequately. In one survey over half the respondents mentioned that they worried about the cost of heating, and a quarter said that this sometimes deterred them from using as much heat as they would like.[3] Central heating is probably the best way of heating an old person's home as it is usually the most economical system, is safer and more convenient than open fires, provides warmth throughout the house (so increasing comfort and helping to maintain the fabric by discouraging condensation), and is less dependent on the old person remembering to switch it on. It is, however, expensive to install. Occasional payments in response to very severe weather are not enough to protect old people from the effects of cold. All people, including the old, should be able to keep their houses at a safe temperature without spending more than 10% of their available income.[4] Many elderly people live in old, poorly maintained houses that are especially hard to heat, and they need help with repairs and insulation as well as with fuel bills.

Safety

Home safety is especially important for elderly people because poor eyesight, restricted mobility, and deteriorating memory increase the risk of accidents; and isolation may delay the arrival of help.

In Britain people aged over 65 have about three million falls each year.[5] Falls are a common reason for admitting old people to hospital, and relatives often pressurise them to move house because of the risk of a further fall. One study of elderly people applying for admission to residential care found that relatives placed far more importance on the risk of falls than did the old people themselves.[6] Studies of falls in elderly people have identified many risk factors including undetected eye and foot disorders, postural hypotension, sudden changes in light intensity, loose rugs, and even poor balance in flat shoes after a lifetime of wearing high heels.[5 7] If old people cannot get up after a fall there should be some sort of alarm system for calling help, which might be nothing more elaborate than a missed regular telephone call to a relative.

In recent years the amount of violent crime against old people in their homes has increased. Health workers are partly to blame for the vulnerability of old people to such attacks. We expect elderly people to leave their front doors open so that we can gain access easily, and few of us offer any identification. Attitudes like these make old people too willing to trust visitors to their homes.

Choice is important

Some houses are more easily adapted for old people than others. Stairs present an obvious hazard, but badly designed bathrooms and kitchens also pose problems for people with restricted movement or poor balance.[8 9] The Centre for Applied Gerontology at the University of Birmingham conducts consumer tests of products designed for elderly people, and its recommendations include hanging kitchen units on brackets like those used for shelving systems so that an entire kitchen can be adapted quickly for wheelchair use, positioning electricity sockets at waist height and fitting plugs with handles, making all doorways wide enough for wheelchair access, installing lever taps, and providing a separate shower as well as a bath. Occupational therapists can provide aids to help old people to cope at home, but if the house is well designed to start with this task is made much easier.

Despite all that can be done to make homes safer and more comfortable, many old people decide to move to specialist housing for the elderly. More options exist now than ever before, ranging from nursing homes and traditional sheltered flats to new continuing care communities. These schemes, which have become very popular in the United States, provide a range of specially designed accommodation on a single site. Old people buy into the scheme and are guaranteed accommodation for life. These complexes are marketed as providing non-institutional, high quality care for the discerning elderly consumer, but in the United States some schemes are now facing problems as the fit people who bought in some years ago are becoming more dependent.

Many old people pay no attention to their housing needs until a sudden illness leaves them unable to cope. Hasty decisions are then forced on them at a time of crisis. Few old people realise the financial implications of moving into specialist housing. Many assume that having sold their own home to gain a residential place they then have tenure for life. It is a bitter blow to find that a further deterioration in health can force them to move again when they have no resources and so no bargaining power over what happens to them. Doctors could do more to explain the implications of normal aging and present housing policy to their elderly patients so that more of them can choose where and how they live.

Housing for the disabled

Disabled people also need a choice of accommodation but have even less choice available to them than the elderly. I have already suggested that elderly people need special provision only if they are in some way disadvantaged, but at least when they do need

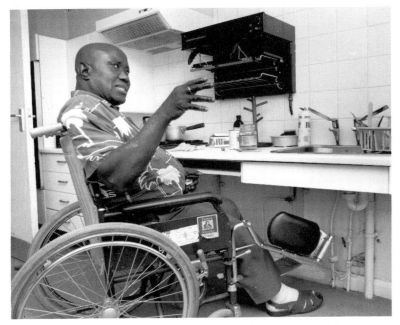

There is a shortage of suitable accommodation for young disabled people

specialist housing there is a long tradition of catering for their needs, and so a reasonable amount of choice. Very little suitable accommodation exists for younger people with mental and physical disabilities, and the recent emphasis on community care has had little impact on the provision of services.

Over 400 000 people aged 16–65 in Britain have a severe physical disability, and about three quarters of them live in the community, depending largely on informal carers for their basic needs.[10] It is now government policy to close many long stay mental hospitals, and the displaced patients are also seeking homes in the community. More and more disabled people are now living in the community, and if they are not given appropriate support their homes can become one of their greatest handicaps.

The challenge in community care is to provide appropriate supporting services without stigmatising the recipients. Using trendy terms like "clients" instead of "patients" is not enough. It is often simpler and cheaper to provide a package of services on a single site, and many community care schemes are effectively small ghettos of handicapped people. Placing all specialist housing in a small area may make services easy to deliver, but it also makes the residents stand out from the rest of the community.

There are a few good housing schemes for physically and mentally disabled people,[10][11] but as always it is the articulate people or those with good advocates who get the best services, and there is a tremendous inequality of provision, with multiply handicapped people and those from ethnic minorities often missing out. More than three quarters of a million physically handicapped people in Britain are inadequately housed, and the National Federation of Housing Associations estimates that there is a shortage of at least 150 000 purpose built or suitably adapted houses in the public sector. Present housing law adds to the problems. Legislation giving council tenants the right to buy their houses at large discounts has deprived many councils of some of their best housing, including many of the most easily adapted homes. The community charge may discourage people from caring for handicapped relatives at home. Present rules on homelessness mean that local authorities are not responsible for housing people who are voluntarily homeless, even if this is the result of them leaving their accommodation during an exacerbation of a mental illness.[12]

Ideally, community care should provide handicapped people with the rights that the rest of us take for granted. They should be able to choose where and with whom they live, who may enter their home, their furnishings and decorations, what time they get up or go to bed, what they eat, when and where they shop, and so on. Inevitably, however, dependence on other people restricts personal freedom. It is time that an element of realism was reintroduced into discussions about community care—compromise is inevitable and we should concentrate on minimising it rather than persisting in futile attempts to eliminate it.

Rehousing on medical grounds

The poor state of much of Britain's housing stock, the grave shortage of homes to rent, and the demands of groups like the homeless and the disabled make it increasingly difficult for council tenants to arrange rehousing. In many places a medical claim to priority increases the chances of success, and doctors are often asked to support such applications.

All doctors need to know how the rehousing system works. It varies from place to place; these guidelines are based on a survey of 55 local authorities.[13] Because there are too few houses to go round, new applicants for council property and existing tenants requesting a transfer usually face a long wait. Local authorities often try to give priority to applicants on the basis of the time spent on the list or by allocating "points" for factors such as family size, overcrowding, standards of present accommodation, and relevant medical problems.

The survey found that authorities use one or another of four ways of collecting medical information: self reporting, information from general practitioners, information collected by specially trained visitors, and assessment by a housing officer. Once collected, the information is reviewed by a medical assessor, usually a community physician, who advises about whether priority should be awarded.

General practitioners need to be familiar with their local system. They need to know whether information should be provided on a

Doctors are often asked to support applications for rehousing

special form and to whom it should be addressed. This avoids repeated requests for more information. Doctors should also remember that it is the degree of disability, not the specific diagnosis, that matters. Emphasis on diagnoses may even be unhelpful—if council employees screen applications they are unlikely to appreciate that "nervous diseases" mean conditions like multiple sclerosis and Parkinson's disease rather than depression.

Medical priority can be unfair

It is difficult to prove that rehousing has much impact on health. A follow up study in Bolton found that nearly a quarter of people rehoused on medical grounds three years earlier thought that their health had improved as a result, but just over a tenth were still unhappy.[14] Studies of people in Salford applying for rehousing on the grounds of ill health found that they improved after rehousing,[15 16] but there are many biases in such studies. It is impossible for subjects to be blinded to the treatment (rehousing), and because many people may exaggerate their symptoms to gain priority any improvement observed after rehousing may be an artefact.

Medical priority for rehousing can be unfair. One of the studies in Salford found that many of the control group also had neurotic symptoms.[16] The authors concluded that a priority system reduces the chances of rehousing for those who do not make a special claim, regardless of their genuine problems. Once again, it is the articulate and aggressive who gain most.

A medical claim for priority is no guarantee of success. Gray found that less than a twentieth of applications for rehousing on medical grounds were successful.[17] Dr Luise Parsons, acting district medical officer in the Northern region, thinks that the scheme is merely a way of deflecting blame for failure to rehouse away from the local authority. "The bottom line is that we haven't got enough houses."

Doctors are placed in a difficult position when asked for support. It is hard to refuse to try to help a patient, even when you know that your list contains many more deserving cases. Many doctors supply reports for all who request them and salve their consciences with the knowledge that the housing shortage is so great that they are unlikely to have any effect anyway. Others devise schemes to support only the most needy cases without offending anyone: a recent conference heard how one housing authority ignored all of the written requests from a particular doctor unless he also telephoned.

Conclusions and comment

Many people have special housing needs because they are poor or ill or disabled. Schemes that target help at older age groups, without specifying disability, often waste resources that could be used better by younger people. The ideals of community care for the physically handicapped and mentally ill hinge on the provision of good housing. Not enough specially adapted homes exist to cater for the needs of disabled people, and there are too few well maintained houses in the public sector to provide healthy housing for other "special" groups such as families, the poor, the homeless, and the unemployed. There are not enough good houses to go round, and it does not require a medical degree to spot the most needy cases, such as bilateral amputees living in tower blocks. Perhaps doctors should distance themselves from the shambles of prioritising cases and campaign instead for improved standards for all.

1 Department of the Environment. *English house conditions survey 1986.* London: HMSO, 1988.
2 Wicks M. *Old and cold. Hypothermia and social policy.* London: Heinemann, 1978.
3 Savage AV. *Warmth in winter: evaluation of an information pack for elderly people.* Cardiff: University of Wales College of Medicine Research Team for the Care of the Elderly, 1988.
4 Lowry S. Temperature and humidity. *Br Med J* 1989;**299**:1326–8.
5 Gabell A, Simons MA, Nayak USL. Falls in the healthy elderly: predisposing causes. *Ergonomics* 1985;**28**:965–75.
6 Neill J. *Assessing elderly people for residential care: a practical guide.* London: National Institute for Social Work Research Unit, 1989.
7 Livesley B. *Falls in older age. Br Med J* 1984;**289**:568–9.
8 Centre for Applied Gerontology. *The kinder kitchen.* Birmingham: University of Birmingham, 1988.
9 Centre for Applied Gerontology. *The better bathroom.* Birmingham: University of Birmingham, 1988.
10 Fiedler B. *Living options lottery. Housing and support services for people with severe physical disabilities, 1986/88.* London: The Prince of Wales's Advisory Group on Disability, 1988.
11 Wertheimer A. *Housing: the foundation of community care.* London: National Federation of Housing Associations, 1989.

12 Lowry S. Concern for discharged mentally ill patients. *Br Med J* 1989;**298**:209–10.
13 Parsons L. Medical priority for rehousing. *Public Health* 1987;**101**:435–41.
14 Cole D, Farries JS. Rehousing on medical grounds—assessment of its effectiveness. *Public Health* 1986;**100**:229–35.
15 Elton PJ, Packer JM. A prospective randomised trial of the value of rehousing on the grounds of mental ill health. *J Chronic Dis* 1986;**39**:221–7.
16 Elton PJ, Packer JM. Neurotic illness as grounds for medical priority for rehousing. *Public Health* 1987;**101**:233–42.
17 Gray JAM. Housing, health and illness. *Br Med J* 1978;**ii**:100–1.

Health and homelessness

There is nothing new about homelessness in Britain—Engels found no fewer than 50 000 homeless in London alone.[1] But how big is the contemporary problem?

A recent survey found that 751 people were sleeping rough on the streets in 17 of London's boroughs on one night, and that did not include people sleeping in derelict buildings, parks, or car parks.[2] In 1989 local authorities in England accepted that people in no fewer than 126 240 households were homeless (up over 7% on the previous year)—representing, according to the housing charity, Shelter, about 362 300 people. And Shelter estimates that there are two million single homeless people in Britain. Here I

Down and out in 1870

discuss the health problems faced by hom·
ways of providing care.

Born homeless

The number of homes available for ren
by a million in the past 25 years. Legislation giving council ....
the right to buy their homes, often at heavily subsidised prices, has
creamed off some of the better public housing to private owner-
ship, and public sector building has not kept pace with the loss. In
1989 132 051 sales to council tenants were completed, bringing the
total to 977 488 since 1980.

Families with children have a right to housing under part 3 of
the 1985 housing act. But because there are so few public sector
houses available homeless families are often placed temporarily in
bed and breakfast hotels. Not unusually such "temporary" arrangements may last for several years.

Living in a bed and breakfast hotel is not an extended luxury
holiday. It means keeping all of your belongings in one room,
living out of suitcases, and having no privacy. Children are born
and brought up in one room, where they live with the rest of their
family. There is no safe place to play. Washing and cooking
facilities are shared with other families, and there may be nowhere
to store food. If the cooking facilities are several floors away
residents have to choose between eating takeaways, having cold

---

**Families in bed and breakfast
accommodation speak out**

"There's only one cooker between about 130 people . . . and if you
do start cooking and then go back to your room then your dinner
either gets burnt or stolen."

"My daughter has been scalded and other children have had electric
shocks. In your own home you can be careful, have gates across
doorways etc, but in a hotel you've got to put up with other people
being careless."

". . . it is very difficult to do my homework. . . . I try to do my work
on the bed but it's difficult as it sinks down in the middle."[10]

Living in a bed and breakfast hotel is not an extended holiday

meals, or carrying saucepans of hot food up several flights of stairs, often with children in tow.

The adverse effects of these conditions on health have been well documented.[34] Homeless women are twice as likely to have problems and three times as likely to need admission to hospital during pregnancy as other women. A quarter of babies born to mothers living in bed and breakfast accommodation are of low birth weight, compared with a national average of less than 1 in 10. The children are more likely to miss out on their immunisations, and poor sanitation and overcrowding encourage the spread of infections and diarrhoeal illnesses. Good nutrition is almost impossible because of the poor facilities for storing and cooking food. Accidents are common among the children, and their parents often suffer from depression.

Sleeping rough

No one knows how many people sleep on the streets in Britain each night, but it is probably several thousand. Some people choose to live rough, but many drift on to the streets because they cannot cope with personal and financial problems. An increasing number have been discharged from disbanded long stay mental hospitals.[5] High interest rates mean that some people are homeless because they cannot meet their mortgage repayments. In 1987 building societies repossessed 22 930 homes, and in the second half of 1989 58 380 loans were 6–12 months in arrears.

Once on the streets it is hard to keep healthy. The shelter, warmth, and privacy often taken for granted do not exist; good food may be hard to find or expensive; it is almost impossible to keep clean; "minor" illnesses are hard to cure.

Dr Malcolm Weller, a consultant psychiatrist in London, conducted a survey of the homeless people attending the Crisis at Christmas venue in 1986. About a third of the people he examined were psychotic and a quarter had severe physical problems, yet two thirds of them had no contact with medical services. The horrors of street life were well summed up in a recent commentary:

> "What is it like to suffer even from simple diarrhoea when there are no public toilets? . . . What is it like to recover from an amputation while struggling with alcoholism and diabetes when there isn't even a place to store one's insulin, much less a source of a diabetic diet?"[6]

Students and doctors at the mobile clinics run by the Whytham Hall Centre in Maida Vale often see infestations and minor skin conditions complicated by secondary infections. Their residential beds are often used by homeless people who need regular meals, clean conditions, and encouragement to comply with the treatment while they are treated for pulmonary tuberculosis.[7] Understandably, it can be difficult to find a general practitioner willing to take on homeless people; they are often hard to motivate about taking medicines and keeping appointments, and many have psychiatric problems that reduce their cooperation even further. They may well leave the practice catchment area before their old notes have been traced. A dirty, unkempt person in the waiting room may upset other patients and the staff.

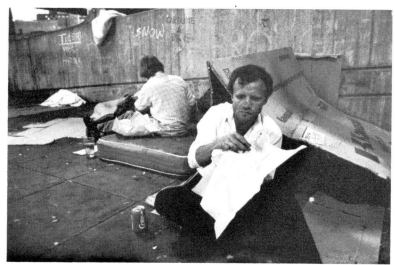

1989—What has changed?

Even so, all the evidence is that homeless people will use facilities provided. The Great Chapel Street clinic in London's Soho is one of several walk in centres providing general practitioner services to homeless people.[8] There is no appointment system, so patients come when they like and are usually well motivated to comply with treatment. And many come back for follow up.

Primary care for the homeless

Schemes such as that at Great Chapel Street do work, but should we be concentrating on special schemes to provide primary care for homeless people? Given that medicine is slowly losing its emphasis on cure and concentrating on prevention, there is a danger that the homeless—who are perhaps most in need of preventive medicine—may miss out because there is no continuity of primary care. Thus the Policy Studies Institute has recently concluded that special services for homeless people may lead to their further isolation, while the range of care offered is less than could be provided by normal services.[9]

Providing a comprehensive health service to mothers and children in bed and breakfast hotels is particularly important. These families are told that the arrangements are temporary, so many do not even try to register with a general practitioner. Many who do try give up after a few rebuffs from doctors unwilling to take on such "problem families," and few realise that the local family practitioner committee will find them a doctor.

One solution, by Dr Richard Stone of the Bayswater Hotel Homeless Project,[10] is to cater specifically for homeless families but to ensure that they have all the benefits of registration with a local doctor. The project pays local general practitioners for sessions at a special surgery. When a family attends it is temporarily registered with the doctor on duty, and after three months permanent registration is arranged.

The Health Visitors Association and the General Medical Services Committee of the BMA have suggested ways of improving primary care for homeless people, including better communication among health workers and using patient held records to improve the continuity of care.[11]

Nevertheless, the changes in the new contract for general practitioners may make it more difficult to provide health care for homeless people—who are not strictly resident in a district; so will their needs be budgeted for? The numerous health and social problems of homeless people make them an unattractive proposition to general practitioners aiming at large lists and a high uptake of immunisation and cervical smear tests.

Hospital care

Even if primary care could be arranged for homeless people the difficulties of access to inpatient services would remain. Hospitals often hide behind catchment area restrictions, and homeless people can end up as no one's responsibility.

Discharging homeless people from hospital is also difficult. Given the increasing pressure to have a rapid turnover of patients, hospitals are increasingly using day case surgery and early discharge to the primary health care team. Yet homeless people often have nowhere to go; sometimes they are discharged to hostels, but these rarely have any medical or nursing supervision.

The London Medical Campaign Project was founded in 1986 after publicity about several homeless patients whose health deteriorated and who died soon after they were discharged from hospital.[12] Trying to coordinate health services for London's homeless, this project has worked with agencies such as the Royal College of General Practitioners and the Royal College of Nursing to educate professionals about their special needs. The campaign runs solely on charitable funding, and the workers find that they have to spend as much time on chasing funds as on working with the homeless.

Conclusions

Homelessness is bad for health. The consequences of life on the streets are all too obvious, but hostel dwellers are often little better off. Living in bed and breakfast accommodation is also damaging to health, yet some of our most vulnerable groups—young children and single mothers—are increasingly being placed in these conditions for months at a time.

There are two main ways of providing health care for homeless people, who need health care as much as anyone else, and often more. Firstly, existing services can be adapted to make them less intimidating and more accessible; secondly, special facilities can be provided. Either of these approaches can be successful when run by an enthusiastic team.

Comment

A few people are homeless because they choose to live that way. Their rejection of organised society makes it unlikely that they will accept mainstream health services, so that some specialist facilities will always be needed, especially in large cities. But many people have not chosen to be homeless. Providing special health services for these people marginalises them further, and it also hides the problem from the providers of mainstream services.

The ideal solution to their problems is an end to homelessness. But how likely is this, given the high interest rates, the paucity of community care for the mentally ill, and the shortage of public sector housing?

Doctors have a duty to speak out about the medical implications of the continuing problem of homelessness—something that no civilised society should accept.

1 Engels F. *Condition of the working class in England in 1844*. London: George Allen and Unwin, 1892.
2 Canter D, Drake M, Littler T, Moore J, Stockley D, Ball J. *The faces of homelessness in London. Interim report to the Salvation Army*. Guildford: Department of Psychology, University of Surrey, 1989.
3 Conway J, ed. *Prescription for poor health. The crisis for homeless families*. London: London Food Commission, Maternity Alliance, SHAC, Shelter, 1988.
4 Howarth V. *A survey of families in bed and breakfast hotels: report to the governors of the Thomas Coram Foundation for Children*. London: Thomas Coram Foundation, 1987.
5 Marshall M. Collected and neglected: are Oxford hostels for the homeless filling up with disabled psychiatric patients? *Br Med J* 1989;**299**:706–9.
6 Hilfiker D. Are we comfortable with homelessness? *JAMA* 1989;**262**:1375–6.
7 Ramsden SS, Baur S, El Kabir DJ. Tuberculosis among the central London single homeless. *J R Coll Physicians Lond* 1988;**22**:16–17.
8 El Kabir DJ. Great Chapel Street Medical Centre. *Br Med J* 1982;**284**:480–1.
9 Williams S, Allen I. *Health care for single homeless people*. London: Policy Studies Institute, 1989.
10 Bayswater Hotel Homelessness Project. *Speaking for ourselves. Families in Bayswater B&B*. London: Bayswater Hotel Homelessness Project, 1987.
11 Health Visitors' Association and General Medical Services Committee. *Homeless families and their health*. London: British Medical Association, 1989.
12 Tyler A. Hospitals spurn homeless. *Time Out* 1985; 5 Dec:12–5.

The cost of homelessness

In the previous chapter I discussed the health effects of homelessness and the difficulties of providing health care to homeless people. These should provide reason enough for correcting the appalling problem of homelessness in Britain, but another disgraceful aspect is the huge drain on financial resources that homelessness represents.

The scale of the problem

In 1989 English authorities agreed that 126 680 households were homeless, and the housing charity Shelter estimates that this represents a national figure of nearly half a million people. But this is only the tip of the iceberg. Among the 1 793 670 applicants who have been refused housing assistance since 1981 are people considered to be intentionally homeless—such as those who have left home to seek work, moved from uninhabitable properties, or been made homeless by rent or mortgage arrears. The figures also exclude the so called "hidden homeless"—people who need a home of their own but are living temporarily with friends or relatives (table I).

TABLE I—*Estimated numbers of homeless people in Britain in 1989*

Officially homeless	162 264
Unofficially homeless:	
Single people	2 000 000
Sleeping rough	6 000
Young people	156 000
"Hidden homeless"	1 200 000

By 2001 nearly 23 million households are likely to exist in Britain, a rise of nearly 2·5 million since 1983. In 1983–7 the number of households on local authority waiting lists for housing increased by 170% and the number housed from the lists decreased by only 14%. The problem is made worse by the increasing number of small (often single person) households, which increases the number of properties needed.

Too few houses

Despite the growing number of housholds, public sector housebuilding is at its lowest level since the war. Local authority investment in housing is in decline (table II), and in London the private rented sector is decreasing at a rate of about 17 000 dwellings a year.[1] In 1978/9 housing took up nearly 7% of all public spending, but by 1989/90 the figure had been cut to about 1·5%.

It is sometimes argued that the housing problem could be solved if the vacant properties in Britain were brought into use. In London alone, about 2900 council properties and 90 000 private sector houses are empty. Though some empty properties un-

Public sector housebuilding is at its lowest ebb since the war

93

TABLE II—*Local authority investment (£ millions) in housing in England[1]*

	Year				
	1980–1	1982–3	1984–5	1986–7	1988–9
London and metropolitan districts	2686	1603	1227	876	672
Non-metropolitan districts in south east	420	389	308	228	150
Other non-metropolitan districts	864	856	610	435	305
Total	3970	2848	2145	1539	1127

doubtedly reflect poor management, all homes cannot possibly be occupied all the time. Some properties are vacant because they are uninhabitable,[2] some may be undergoing repairs or upgrading, and others may be being sold or relet. Upgrading unfit empty homes to a standard that would allow them to be used would be expensive and would not solve the housing shortage.

Effects of housing policy

In recent years the government has encouraged market forces to dictate costs and availability in the rented sector. Local authority rents have risen from an average of £6·40 a week in 1979 to £21 in 1989, but if they had kept pace with rises in the retail price index the average would now be only about £13.[3] Many people are unable to pay these "market rents", and over 4·1 million tenants now rely on the housing benefit system to meet some or all of their rent. This is a huge drain on public funds.

Since 1980, nearly 977 500 council houses in England have been sold to tenants, often at greatly subsidised prices. This has had two effects on homelessness. Because mortgage rates have risen dramatically, many people who bought under the "right to buy" schemes are now unable to meet their repayments and therefore face repossession of their homes. In theory many of these people could then be classed as intentionally homeless, and their local authority would have no further obligation to house them.

The sale of public sector houses has also reduced the stock available to councils for housing homeless people. In theory the receipts from the sale of council homes could create an enormous opportunity for reinvestment, but authorities are only allowed to spend a quarter of receipts from sales on new buildings and renovations.

Under part 3 of the Housing Act 1985, local authorities are obliged to house certain homeless people, including families with children, pregnant women, the old, and those who are mentally or physically infirm. Because of the shortage of permanent homes, such people are often placed in temporary accommodation—hostels, refuges, mobile homes, or the infamous bed and breakfast hotels (table III). The end of the first quarter of 1990 saw 41 170 households living in temporary accommodation—an increase of 34% on the same period in the previous year. In London alone the annual cost of providing temporary accommodation is more than £200 million.

TABLE III—*Average numbers of homeless households placed in temporary accommodation in England in 1984–9*

	Year					
	1984	1985	1986	1987	1988	1989
London and metropolitan districts:						
Bed and breakfast	2 230	2 840	5 216	8 638	8 548	8 368
Other	4 250	4 840	6 083	7 858	11 191	15 058
Non-metropolitan districts:						
Bed and breakfast	790	1 010	1 525	2 150	2 705	3 265
Other	3 930	4 280	4 815	5 315	6 423	8 163
Total	11 200	12 970	17 639	23 961	28 867	34 853

Homelessness wastes money

It costs £14 600 to keep a family in bed and breakfast accommodation in London for one year, and £5475 outside the metropolitan area. A new house for rent could be built for £8200 in London and £5000 elsewhere. The Audit Commission drew attention to this waste of resources recently: "Bed and breakfast hotels usually offer the lowest standards at the highest costs", and called instead for investment in "homes at prices affordable by homeless people."[4] Meanwhile local authorities, which are obliged to sell houses to

95

tenants and are restricted in the amount that they can spend on new building and repairs, are forced to squander resources on expensive temporary accommodation.

Solutions

The government has recently announced a £250 million package to be spent on homelessness over two years. Of this, £112 million has been allocated to specific projects, including £22 million in cash incentives to council tenants to buy homes in the private sector, so releasing council homes for homeless people. The government hopes that the whole scheme will provide 5000 new lettings, but this is a very small contribution given that in 1989 nearly 35 000 homeless households were placed in temporary accommodation by local authorities.

The Town and Country Planning Association has stated that "the private rented sector is simply not geared to providing cheap housing for rent".[5] It wants local authorities to be enabled to build houses for rent based on local need and replace stock lost through sales to tenants.

Conclusions

Too few houses are available for rent at prices affordable by homeless people. Many aspects of recent housing policy have contributed to the increasing problem of homelessness. The "right to buy" legislation has reduced local authority housing stock, and restrictions on the use of capital receipts make it impossible to replace the lost homes, much less meet future increased needs. Local authorities are not even able to make adequate repairs to their remaining properties. High interest rates are forcing many families into debt and, eventually, homelessness.

Comment

If council tenants are to continue to have a right to buy their homes the current market value of the property should determine the price and the authority should be obliged to reinvest most of the receipts in its housing stock. If necessary, money should be allocated to prime the pump for a new wave of public sector house building. That would eventually free authorities from the vicious circle of having to spend so much on temporary housing that no money is left for the only possible solution to the present crisis—more homes.

1 Oldman J. *Who says there's no housing problem? Facts and figures on housing and homelessness.* London: Shelter, 1990.
2 Department of the Environment. *English house condition survey 1986.* London: HMSO, 1988.
3 Oldman J. *Temporary accommodation: the permanent story.* London: Shelter, 1990.
4 Audit Commission. *Housing the homeless: the local authority role.* London: Audit Commission, 1989.
5 Town and Country Planning Association. *Whose responsibility? Reclaiming the inner cities.* London: Town and Country Planning Association, 1986.

Getting things done

Despite building regulations and public health laws many people in Britain still live in conditions that would have been familiar to the Victorians. In this final chapter I examine how the residents of two of the worst housing estates in Britain have tried to put things right.

Divis

The Divis flats have been described as "the youngest slum in Europe," yet ironically they were built as part of Belfast's slum clearance programme in the 1960s to replace mill workers' houses in the Old Pound Loney district.[1] There was religious and political pressure to keep the old community intact, and the planners devised a system of 13 seven storey deck access blocks and a 19 storey tower block, providing accommodation for nearly 3000 people on the old site in an area of 6025 hectares (14·8 acres).

The developers in Divis, as in other parts of Britain, were offered subsidies to use new building techniques, and by the early 1970s the residents were noticing problems now known to be common in such systems built properties. Cracks in the cladding, poorly constructed joints, ill fitting windows, cold bridging between slabs, and poor insulation made the flats cold and damp. Flat roofs encouraged penetrating damp. Asbestos had been widely used for insulation, including blue asbestos rope around the window panels. Calcium chloride had been added to the cement to speed the drying time, and when the concrete later cracked water penetrated and chloride ions attacked the steel supporting beams. There were problems with the sewerage system, and flooding was common. Rats and cockroaches colonised cracks in the structure.

The residents in Divis suffered the emotional strains found in

Divis—the youngest slum in Europe

similar blocks across Britain. Poor maintenance added to the squalor, and young mothers and old people were especially isolated. Unemployment and poverty were rife. Added to these problems was the additional strain of living in a politically sensitive part of Northern Ireland. The Divis complex is a nationalist

99

stronghold. Many of its residents have been interned, some have been shot, and the complex has been the scene of several pitched battles with the army. There is a constant military presence in the area, including frequent helicopter surveillance, and homes are often raided and searched.

In 1986 the Divis Joint Development Committee, a voluntary group of local residents and social workers, commissioned a survey of the health of residents.[2] Conditions in Divis were compared with those in the Twinbrook estate in west Belfast. Twinbrook consists mainly of houses with gardens—but, like Divis, it is a deprived area. At the time of the survey 82% of adults and 85% of children in Twinbrook were living in poor households (with an income of 140% of the supplementary benefit rate) compared with 96% of adults and children in Divis.

A questionnaire was used to collect information about health, and major differences were found between the two estates. Respiratory and gastrointestinal illnesses were more often reported in children from Divis, and nearly a third of children had been seen by a general practitioner during the previous month, compared with less than a tenth of those in Twinbrook. Adults in Divis were about four times as likely to report that their health was poor as those in Twinbrook and nearly twice as many in Divis had a longstanding medical problem.

The study had been commissioned to further the struggle for better housing, but in the end one of the main disadvantages of living in Divis (the political situation) proved the key to success. Since the late '60s the residents had wanted total demolition of the complex, but the Northern Ireland Housing Executive favoured rehabilitation of the blocks. Official reports estimated that rehabilitation would cost £5 m and extend the life of the blocks by 15 years. Total replacement would cost £15 m, and the new houses would last 60 years. Heated exchanges between the residents and the housing executive led, in 1970, to the offer of a compromise: demolition of two blocks, rehabilitation of 11, and the building of 100 new houses, at a total cost of £8 m. But the residents continued to demand total demolition.

In 1979 the Divis Demolition Committee was formed. This group of residents organised a campaign of wrecking flats as they became empty in an attempt to force the housing executive to meet their demands. The campaign received a boost in 1981 when three ringleaders pleaded guilty in court to charges of causing malicious damage, and the judge gave only a nominal fine.

In 1985 the Town and Country Planning Association mounted an exhibition in London about conditions in Divis. This caused an outcry in the national and international press. In October 1986 the Northern Ireland housing minister announced that all of the deck access blocks in Divis would be demolished and the residents rehoused. The official explanation for the decision was economic, but political embarrassment caused by international publicity about the appalling conditions in Divis must have had some influence. "The troubles" may have been a strain on the residents of Divis, but they also allowed poor housing to become a political issue.

Easthall

A survey by the City of Glasgow District Council in 1987 found that nearly a third of the city's houses were damp.[3] More than half had no central heating, and less than a quarter had full central heating. Almost a third of Glasgow's council tenants could not afford to run the heating installed in their homes.

Easthall, part of the Easterhouse area of north east Glasgow, has had more than its share of problems with damp, but it also has an active residents' association that is determined to put things right. In 1984 they set up a Dampness Group which discovered that many homes in the area were badly affected. Local residents were disheartened by the failure of the housing department to take any effective action in response to complaints. The best that happened was a temporary repair job with fungicidal washes, which worked for about three months, or dry lining of the walls, which camouflaged the problems for about a year.

The residents commissioned the Technical Services Agency to find out what was causing the dampness and whether it could be cured.[4] A survey disclosed that many of the houses were not brick buildings, as the residents had believed, but Wilson blocks—two leaves of concrete with metal ties between them. Damaged joints between the blocks of concrete had allowed water to permeate by capillary action, and moisture had crossed many of the integral ties and soaked the inner walls. The insulation properties of these houses were very poor, and it could cost up to £50 a week to heat

101

them adequately. (Residents in Easthall cannot afford to spend this much on heating; but even by restricting the amount of heat used most spend about £15 each week on fuel.)

The residents had also been concerned by large cracks in the walls of their homes, and exploratory digs confirmed that the buildings had moved on their foundations. Full surveys confirmed a diagonal crack on the third floor walls in all of the Wilson block houses, and this was attributed to the use of a poor mix of concrete. Poor maintenance of window frames, roofs, and gutters throughout the estate added to the problems.

In 1985 the residents presented the results of their study to the housing department of Glasgow district council, and the long battle for action began. The council agreed in principle that something should be done, but said that there was no money available. In the months that followed the residents had many unproductive meetings with officials and gradually accumulated a mass of evidence including photographs, maps, plans, and temperature profiles that they combined into a poster presentation. By mounting this exhibit at public meetings the residents were able to generate a great deal of badly needed publicity.

In 1987 the residents hit on their most effective scheme for generating interest and action. A "Heatfest"was organised in association with the Scottish Solar Energy Group, the West of Scotland Energy Working Group, the Technical Services Agency, and Glasgow district council. Architects, surveyors, engineers, housing managers, and tenants' representatives from all over Britain attended three days of seminars and workshops culminating in a competition for the best solution to Easthall's problems.

The winning scheme incorporates a glazed buffer space behind the kitchens and bathrooms. This could be used for washing and drying clothes, so removing a source of condensation from the main part of the house. Existing verandas would be enclosed and glazed, and solar panels would collect heat and direct it to the stairwells. Heat collected from solar panels or special roof tiles could also be used to preheat water, so reducing fuel bills. Insulation of the external walls would reduce heat loss, and gas central heating would provide the most economical heat source.

The planners calculated that the "Heatfest house" would provide value for money. The current expected lifespan of the Wilson blocks is about 15 years, but the proposed scheme would add a

Wilson block houses in Easthall

further 20 years at a unit cost of £15 000–17 000. Because fuel bills would drop to about £7 a week tenants could afford some rent increases that would help to meet the capital costs.

The winning package was offered a European Community grant of £400 000 as a passive solar demonstration project. Such grants are expected to cover 40% of the cost of demonstration projects, so the Easthall residents looked to Glasgow district council for the balance. The council had participated in the Heatfest and had mentioned the scheme in its own press releases as part of the World

Health Organisation's healthy cities project, but it was slow to find the money needed. During the summer of 1989 it looked as though the residents might lose their opportunity, as the offer had a time limit. They learnt only in January 1990 that the council would provide £950 000, enough for a three year demonstration project of 36 houses. The scheme will be monitored by the Mackintosh School of Architecture in Glasgow, which will report to the European Commission, and the residents also intend to monitor the health of people in the Heatfest houses.

Comment

Studies of the effects of housing on health are complicated by confounding variables such as poverty, unemployment, and social class. It is not always obvious what should be measured, or how, or when. Self reported results may be biased, but objective measurements may underestimate effects. Standards that are acceptable for most people may be too lax for vulnerable groups like the elderly and children.

It is difficult to prove that housing harms health as defined by a

New two storey houses are replacing the old blocks in Divis—why not elsewhere too?

strictly medical model, but if we choose the World Health Organisation's concept of health as a state of emotional and physical wellbeing[5] the effects are obvious. Modern medicine is as much about prevention as cure, and doctors have a role in campaigning for better housing conditions in Britain. Providing more and better housing is a cost effective way of improving people's health.

Easthall is typical of estates all over Britain. The residents have known for years that their living conditions are harming their health, but action is rarely taken on the basis of such claims. The residents have shown initiative and suggested a cost effective solution to their problems, but official help has been slow.

Conditions in Divis are bad, but they are no worse than in many other parts of Britain. Yet the old blocks are being demolished and new two storey houses are already taking their place. Officially this is the result of sound economic reasoning, so why are the economics so often ignored elsewhere? It should not be necessary to harness campaigns for good housing to political embarrassments like the tragedy of Northern Ireland before the government is shamed into action.

1 Graham D. *The Divis report. Set them free.* Belfast; Divis Residents' Association, 1986.
2 Blackman T, Evason E, Melaugh M, Woods R. *Housing and health in west Belfast. A case study of Divis Flats and the Twinbrook estate.* Belfast: Divis Joint Development Committee, 1987.
3 Robertson DS. Attacking the dampness plague: Glasgow's response. *Health Promotion* 1989;4:159–62.
4 Easthall Residents' Association. *Easthall—hard to heat, hard to beat.* Glasgow: Community Resources Project, Glasgow College of Technology, 1987.
5 World Health Organisation. *Alma-Ata 1978; primary health care.* Geneva: WHO, 1978. (Health for all series. No 1.)

Index

SOCIAL SCIENCE LIBRARY

Manor Road Building
Manor Road
Oxford OX1 3UQ
Tel: (2)71093 (enquiries and renewals)
http://www.ssl.ox.ac.uk

This is a NORMAL LOAN item.

We will email you a reminder before this item is due.

Please see http://www.ssl.ox.ac.uk/lending.html
for details on:

- loan policies; these are also displayed on the notice boards and in our library guide.

- how to check when your books are due back.

- how to renew your books, including information on the maximum number of renewals.
Items may be renewed if not reserved by another reader. Items must be renewed before the library closes on the due date.

- level of fines; fines are charged on overdue books.

Please note that this item may be recalled during Term.